Be y... the world is waiting!

A Guide to Getting It:

Sacred Healing

Laura Biering

Lynn Bieber • Laura Biering • Rick Garrison
Lisa Guyman • Pam Hillinger • Beth Kopitzke
Lisa Matzke • Alexis McKenna • Lisa Morgan
Marilyn Schwader • Kathleen Thompson

Marilyn Schwader, Editor

CLARITY OF VISION PUBLISHING • PORTLAND, OREGON

Other books in the series:
A Guide to Getting It: Self-Esteem
A Guide to Getting It: Achieving Abundance
A Guide to Getting It: Remarkable Management Skills
A Guide to Getting It: A Clear, Compelling Vision
A Guide to Getting It: Powerful Leadership Skills

For more information, visit www.ClarityOfVision.com
To order any of the *A Guide to Getting It* book series, visit
www.AGuideToGettingIt.com

BOOK DESIGN AND PRODUCTION BY MARILYN SCHWADER

ISBN 0-9716712-5-7
Library of Congress Control Number: 2004110927
First edition: January 2005

Table of Contents

Acknowledgments

I am fortunate to have had many teachers guiding me to an understanding and recognition of my own *Sacred Healing*. Thank you to all of the friends, family, and coaches who have contributed to my physical, mental, emotional, and spiritual growth. And a very grateful thank you to the authors who have contributed their knowledge and experience in the writing of this book. Your talents as healers and your ability to express your experience and ideas to others has ripple effects throughout the fabric of the universe. We are all better because of your work.

Marilyn Schwader, Editor

A Note from the Editor

Sacred Healing offers timeless, profound, compelling, and transforming information for those who are seeking healing in all aspects of their life—mental, emotional, spiritual, and physical. The chapters in this book help people discover a life abundant in rewards: integration, sanctuary, vibrancy, and spirituality. The contributing authors have written chapters with simple, thought-provoking ideas and stories that will help you have a healthier, happier, and more fulfilling life.

This book is the sixth book in a series of books written by Life and Business Coaches to help the reader improve their business and personal life. I invite you to read, explore, and enjoy!

Marilyn Schwader, Editor

The Flow of Life:
Fearing Less and Loving More

By Marilyn Schwader

"Everyone has two choices. We're either full of love, or full of fear." ~ Albert Einstein

I looked back over the seat of my loaded-to-the-gills car toward the building on the corner of the street. What I saw as I prepared to drive away was the end of my life's dream. The restaurant I had created was closing its doors. I had packed all of my personal items in the car, and in a few minutes, the auctioneer would start to sell the pieces of equipment that had served so many in the five years I had struggled to make the business succeed.

I couldn't stay and watch as the baby I had birthed, coaxed through infancy, dragged through puberty, and prodded into adolescence was sold piece by piece to unknown faces who circled like vultures. The hurt was too great, and with tears blurring my vision, I started the car and drove away.

Prior to creating the restaurant, my life had been full of wonderful experiences, joyful relationships, and charmed work situations. I had experienced loss, but nothing so devastating, and so tangible. Added to the sorrow was hearing time and again that what I had built had been successful for employees and customers in every way—except for that most important of criteria: the bottom line.

How could I have gone from such promise and accomplishment in creating a beautiful, nourishing space, to losing everything? I had followed my intuition to accomplish my dream, and optimism and a clear sense of purpose had propelled me to build that business. Fear had destroyed it. And fear would continue to enter into my life as I stumbled through the aftermath of regret, frustration, and despair. My life had taken a sharp turn from happiness and contentment to misery and a feeling of abject failure.

I lost my business, my house, a long-term relationship, and along with those, my self-esteem, my belief in my abilities, my openness to possibilities, and ultimately my health. Between the depression I fell into, the back spasms and physical discomfort caused by not caring for my body, and the daily pity-party I gave myself, I was a mess.

To alleviate the pain, I began to drink and remained in a drug-induced stupor most days. Thinking a change of scenery would alter my state of affairs, I decided to move to another state. And instead of taking time to heal, I jumped into another relationship. I didn't explore what I needed to fix about myself, and in a short time lost that most valuable of commodities—trust—in my intuition, in others, in the universe. Like a snowball picking up layers as it rolls down a hill, the choices I made continued to attract trouble.

After four years of tumbling down that steep terrain, I was desperate. I had isolated myself from my friends and family during that time, and began to have a deep longing to surround myself with those who steadfastly looked beyond my failings and the judgments that I heaped on myself. I decided that for the holidays, I would drive back to Oregon to see some familiar faces. My partner and I packed the car and headed out of Santa Fe three days before Christmas. While I was excited, I also carried a feeling of shame that I wasn't where I thought I'd be in my life. Although my closest friends and my family had never stopped offering their support, I couldn't see how they could still have respect for me. I didn't have it for myself, so why should anyone else?

My partner and I were having difficulties, and the relationship had gone from so-so to bad. My financial difficulties had followed me, and I was full of anger and hate aimed at those who had seemingly helped in the demise of my business. I was unhappy about so many things in my life, at times I just wanted to end it all. Those thoughts crept in more and more. As we drove through

Utah on our way to the Northwest, I imagined what it would be like to fall asleep at the wheel and die in a car wreck. As I thought about the possibility, I found myself ready to leave the miserable existence I was living. The only reason I didn't drive off the road and kill myself at that moment was that I carried another life in the vehicle. So, I reluctantly let go of the idea, and continued driving, regretting that I wasn't traveling solo.

The next day, the universe answered my request. At least, part of it. I fell asleep at the wheel, and we went into a horrific rollover at 85 miles per hour, tumbling seven times before we came to a stop. Truly, a "be careful what you ask for" moment. Miraculously, we not only survived, we climbed out of the vehicle under our own power and walked away with one scratch, a couple of concussions, a wide-open view of how life can change in an instant, and a new understanding that when the universe wants to, it can hit you over the head with a two-by-four.

I woke up that day. I didn't know exactly what I was waking up to at that point. That took a few months to sink in through the concussion. But, as I walked away from the destroyed vehicle and laid down on the side of the road to await the ambulance, I knew at a deep level that I had been given an opportunity to see a new perspective, and more important, to change my response to how I lived in that perception.

One of the first outcomes of the accident was that I lost my fear—of beginnings and endings, of change, of success and failure, of living—and of dying. Once I had faced death, nothing in life seemed insurmountable. Of course, I always had the option of becoming more fearful. That choice exists for all of us. For reasons that have since become clear to me, in the aftermath of the accident I made the decision that I would no longer respond to life from fear, but to come from a place of openness and love. And that, as Robert Frost said so eloquently in his poem, has made all the difference.

Coming from Love versus Fear

Fear and love. The two most powerful emotions we humans experience—and the most significant duality in our universe. I was born with what a good friend calls the "happy gene." My family calls me an optimist, and it was a well-known fact that I always looked for the silver lining in any cloud that formed. Until I was in the throes of running the restaurant, I operated almost exclusively from a place of love. I was very trusting, very open, and thought good things of others, regardless of how they might think of me.

But shortly after the restaurant opened, I was jolted into an unfamiliar space after a good friend betrayed my trust and sought to destroy what I had helped to create. For the first time in my life, I was faced with the unfamiliar feeling of mistrust, a product of fear. Once that seed of fear is planted, the roots can take hold quickly. The betrayal set a series of events in motion that began to affect my confidence and my choices. My "logical" brain took over, and I began to ignore the intuitive hits that kept coming in on a daily basis. I began to exude a fearful energy, and more reasons to fear came into my life. The law of attraction works both ways, from love or fear. As I operated from anxiety, dread, and alarm, more consequences of those emotions came into my life.

Breaking the Pattern:
The Seven C's of Transformation

Ironically, for years prior to and during the restaurant, I had talked about a model of listening to your intuition that I call, "Breaking the Pattern: The Seven C's of Transformation." I created this model after I started seeing patterns in my life, and began to look at what might cause me to repeat harmful behavior. Although I was obviously aware of elements of how we respond to life's decision-making process, I hadn't experienced all the levels that I included in the model. I just *thought* I had. Then I had my car accident. And I saw clearly how my pattern of denying my intuitive voice had brought me to that turning point. When I moved away from following my intuition, fear took a foothold. As fear grew, change became even more difficult. The negative energy continued to expand and attract more negative energy. Ultimately, the result of my refusal to pay attention to those all-important signals had disastrous results.

Let me explain how this works. The Seven C's of Transformation are:

- Conscious Awareness
- Concern
- Critical Mass
- Crisis
- Chaos
- Choice
- Change

First, there is **Conscious Awareness**, when our subconscious meets our conscious. This is that first inkling, when we hear an internal voice, or our body responds to something to get our attention. This is our intuition starting a dialogue with us. For many reasons, societal, cultural, or familial, we have moved away from following our intuition. But, in that moment of Conscious Awareness, we have a **Choice** to look at the message we are receiving and make a **Change** in the course of the event we are experiencing. If we are in tune with what's happening, we will make the Change and the inkling goes away. If not, the Conscious Awareness elevates to **Concern**.

Concern is when the intuitive voice gets a little bit louder. We start to squirm a bit, and our body gets more agitated. Not choosing to change begins to be uncomfortable. Again, if we tune in to the intuitive signs and make the change, the troubling signs will disappear. However, most of us still ignore the Concerned feeling and choose to stay the course. Most often this is due to our logical brains telling us that following our intuition doesn't "make sense." Or we continue to hope things will change on their own, so *we* don't have to implement the Change.

When we continue to ignore the signs, we reach the point of **Critical Mass**. Despite the dire sound of this stage, it is not the end of the process. If we choose to change the course of how we got to this point, the intuition is satisfied and it will stop sending the urgent messages. And yet, most of us continue to ignore the signs, even at this level of discomfort. And so we move to **Crisis**.

A significant portion of our population lives in the Crisis stage, sometimes for months or years, continually denying that Change is necessary. I lived in Crisis for nearly seven years, ignoring every piece of information that told me that Change was not only necessary, it was absolutely essential to my well-being. Denial is not a river in Egypt. But I was layered in it. More indications from my internal sources (mental, emotional, and physical responses) continued to indicate that Change was necessary. And yet, I maintained a relentless belief that I couldn't or didn't have the ability to make the necessary changes to break the pattern. Humans can maintain this posture indefinitely, but the toll on our bodies and minds is tremendous. Fighting our intuition is truly the fight of our life at this stage. And our intuition is always right. So although we think we are winning the battle, we are losing the war.

Despite our best attempts at trying to influence the ways we receive, interpret, and control the message, the universe has its own methods of helping us see our way to our divine purpose. Ignoring, fighting, or denying the intuition's existence and importance is done so with great peril to our physical and spiritual well-being. This is true because intuition is the voice of guidance that leads us on the path of fulfilling our destiny. While we may *believe* that not following that voice works, in the end, the forces of the universe will overpower our ego, and ultimately cause the **Chaos** that precedes the existence of order.

Some people I've shared this model with believe that they are in Chaos, not Crisis. Here's the difference: we can stay in Crisis indefinitely; it's a "stage." Chaos is a very short, very precise, and very direct event that we have absolutely no control over, and which, in the end, literally turns our world upside down. This can take the form of someone being caught doing something illegal, a house burning, a serious illness, and yes—a car accident. The accumulation of energy from our inaction, our ego's relentless attachment to the outcome, or our fear of changing what we know so well, even though it's dangerous to our health and well-being, will eventually build to the point that Chaos will inevitably occur.

Chaos nearly always causes us to make that Change that will bring us peace. However, some people continue to repeat the patterns, still not willing to embrace that their life would improve radically if they did. Those people are harmful to themselves and others, and will likely push themselves to a quick demise, whether by illness, accident, or violence. Operating from fear has become a way of life for them. They cannot see a way out of their current existence. They have completely denied their intuitive voice.

Intuition and the Flow of Life

"THE INTELLECT HAS LITTLE TO DO ON THE ROAD TO DISCOVERY. THERE COMES A LEAP IN CONSCIOUSNESS, CALL IT INTUITION OR WHAT YOU WILL, AND THE SOLUTION COMES TO YOU, AND YOU DON'T KNOW HOW OR WHY." ~ALBERT EINSTEIN

Intuition occurs naturally when you are living in a fluid way, detached from worries, "shoulds," and strong opinions and belief systems. The flow of life is a very simple pattern of movement. Imagine a funnel. Below the funnel is the subconscious, where inspiration is born. Where conscious and subconscious meet is what we refer to as intuition. At that point we have a Conscious Awareness, a creative "seed" is planted. As that idea grows in our consciousness, it begins to manifest into reality. Once manifested, our soul's needs are filled and we begin the process again. When we are at rest or asleep, our superconscious, or higher power, transfers new information and new energy to our subconscious, and the process continues its cycle. This is happening all of the time in each of us.

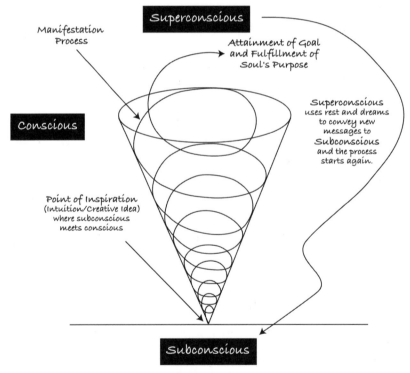

The Flow of Life Funnel

That's why I firmly believe that we can all be in the flow of life. However, when we come from a place of fear, we place layers of belief and filters of doubt in the way of manifesting the soul's higher purpose. We can choose to allow those filters to block the manifestation process—or we can choose to remove those blocks and allow the flow to continue.

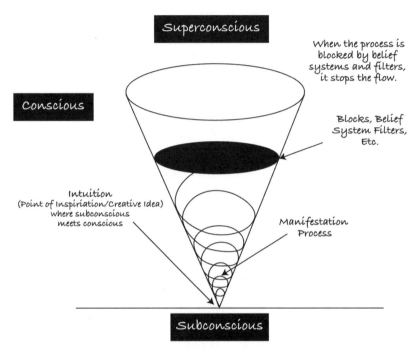

The Flow of Life Funnel Blocked

Do you have control over what will and will not ultimately manifest? I don't believe you do. Because it's your soul's higher purpose to manifest your divine destiny. You can try all you want to alter the course, to stop the movement, to control the forces, to fear the direction your life might be taking you. But, you must eventually reach your soul's higher purpose. Despite your attempts, the universe has ultimate influence, and you will eventually be given a reminder of the power of your destiny. The more you ignore your intuition and the signals it sends, the more you will struggle, and the more disease, pain, and distress will enter into your life. However, you can choose to:

- claim the moment
- let go of the expectation of an outcome
- understand your beliefs and the effect they have on the process
- remove the filters that keep you from easily manifesting your soul's higher purpose
- allow the process to occur

Claim the Moment

One of my healing teachers and I were talking one day. I was proudly telling her that I had recently been learning patience through several lessons that had been appearing in my life. Because I had always been led to believe that patience was a virtue, I was willingly taking on the assignments, although the episodes had been difficult and caused me various types of pain, both emotional and physical. She stopped me at that point and said, "Marilyn, be careful what language you are using to describe these instances. The spirits live in the moment. They are not looking at what you've done in the past or what the future is. If you ask for patience, they will give you reasons to have patience. Instead, say, 'I'm claiming the moment.' "

Language is powerful. And what we say and think has a significant impact on how we move in and through our lives. What we tell ourselves is a huge part of how we manifest things in our lives and has a direct affect on our health. I suggest to my clients that they do the following exercise for one day. I have them write a hash mark each time they catch themselves saying (aloud or internally) anything that comes from a place of fear, is negative, judgmental, or pessimistic. At the end of the day, I have them count up all the hash marks. Even those who believe their communication is positive are amazed at how many times their language fails them.

When you find yourself fearing the future or agonizing over the past, say to yourself, "I'm claiming this moment."

It's a reminder to stay present, to release control, and to exult in the here and now.

Let Go of the Expectation of an Outcome

I remember times growing up when I would imagine myself in situations, for example a party I might be preparing to attend, and become very anxious about what I might say, or how I would be perceived, or who might like me—or not. I would build elaborate stories in my mind, some good, some bad. Inevitably when I attended the event, I would be disappointed, sometimes because what I imagined didn't come true—and sometimes because it did. What a miserable way to be. I would expect an outcome and always be thoroughly dismayed when it didn't happen. Even when an outcome that I desired did happen, I was still often disappointed, because it was usually not as good as I hoped. My expectations just couldn't be met.

A couple of years ago, as I prepared to go home to South Dakota for a family event, I was planning my schedule, making an agenda, and driving myself crazy trying to fit everything into the time I would be there. I sat down on the edge of the bed and took a deep breath. The realization hit me that if I didn't have to meet anyone's expectations the trip would be a lot more joyful. Then I had an even deeper realization that if I didn't have expectations, or an agenda, or even a schedule, that the trip would be a breeze. I decided to try it. I allowed other people to make their schedules, and told them that, if possible, when they let me know the time and place, I'd be there. Even when it was last minute, I didn't care. In fact, last minute plans eliminated my creating outcomes in my mind. I just showed up, with no expectations.

The result was astounding. I floated through the 10 days. I was filled with joy. There were no promises that might be broken, no drama from having made plans that someone else didn't like, and with no expectations, I was never disappointed. By the end of the trip, everyone was asking me how I could remain so calm and happy when things seemed to be swirling around my large and loud family.

After that experience, I started to do that in my day-to-day life. Spontaneity has become very fun. When something comes up, I check with my intuition, stay present, and make the decision in the moment. Then I refrain from attaching expectations to the outcome, and as a result, am not disturbed by what might happen.

Understand Your Beliefs and Their Influence

What influences whether we listen to our intuition? Why do we deny our intuition and ignore the physical, mental, emotional, and spiritual signs along the way? The greatest impact on our decision-making is our belief system. The influence on our beliefs comes from our experiences, who we choose to listen to, who we are sometimes indoctrinated to believe, and who we might aspire to revere.

I recently heard an analogy that John Welwood described in his book *Love and Awakening*. When you are born, you are given a beautiful castle with hundreds of rooms, each representing a part of your inner world. The rooms are perfect, and each contains a gift. As a child, you explore each room with no preconceived ideas, no shame, no judgment. As you get older, you start hearing from others that certain rooms are not right, that you should lock them up to keep the castle safe. Because you desire acceptance and love, you close the room. Then another, and another. You stop listening to your inner voice and instead believe the opinions of others. In no time, you are living in a one-bedroom house in need of repairs.

I believe that we are all born with the same amount of joy in our hearts. We each begin our life with openness and come from a place of love. How we choose to respond to the voices we hear, the belief systems that are thrust upon us, will determine which rooms of our house we close and which stay open. When we come from fear, more rooms will remain closed. Love keeps the doors open.

Fear is not a bad thing, unless it becomes paralyzing. Fear can protect you from harm—and it can also keep you from enjoying the flow of life.

For some reason in our culture, looking for the good in things, being positive, being fearless, has become a negative thing. Have you ever had someone say to you that you are not being "realistic"? How is it that being negative and coming from a place of fear is more realistic than being open and loving? According to estimates, 90% of what we worry about never happens. If negative worries have a 10% chance of occurring, doesn't that mean that being positive is more realistic? The important thing to ask yourself is why it's better to be fearful when you have a choice not to be. After all, you have the same ability to choose love as you do to choose fear.

Remove the Filters

As I mentioned earlier, one of the most powerful means of change is language. Another significant method is visualization. Imagine your own funnel of manifestation. What filters (some people call them Gremlins, or voices of fear, etc.) keep you from moving toward your purpose? Picture them blocking the funnel. Then imagine yourself removing them, one by one. Slide them out and allow the next moment to happen, without expectation. Allow the process to occur, instead of trying to control it. Free yourself from limiting beliefs and the idea that you aren't good enough. Regain your trust—in you and in the universe and that which is your purpose, your destiny.

Allow the Process to Occur

The "C" word that doesn't appear in my "Breaking the Pattern" model is **Control**. This aspect is often overlooked in the discussion of fear. In my experience, when something negative happens to us, particularly at a young age, we seek ways to make our environment safe, or to make others conform to our ideas, or to maintain a semblance of order. This need for control is a direct response to fear. In fact, it is the single most influential belief that compels us to ignore our intuition.

Allowing the process to occur requires letting go of the idea that we have, or more importantly, *need* to have control. Is that need really serving you? How much energy do you expend trying to maintain an outward appearance of control? When you get out of your own way and the flow begins to happen, you will see that all the energy you've expended on controlling the process or the outcome will begin to serve you, instead of blocking you from what you want in your life. Let go of an outcome, remove the filters, and allow the process to occur. Your inner voice will guide you if you allow it.

Choosing Less Fear and More Love

Along with the duality of love and fear, the universal source also saw fit to give us free will. Choice is a blessing, and can also be a curse, because every decision made has an outcome, and we humans, with our egos in tow, have come to believe that we have control of both the process and the outcome. That feeling of control over our lives drives us to denial when we face a fearful event. This is true, even on an infinitesimal scale—when even awareness becomes a reason to judge, a reason to doubt, to make up stories, to cast aside trust. In that fear we begin to grasp for what is safe, comfortable, and familiar.

Choice has impacted every aspect of our lives. Look around at what you have in your life. Outside of nature, every object and every person in our lives exists because someone chose to act one way instead of another. Those who have created, inspired, and taken positive leadership roles have moved past their fears, acted with openness to an idea, and allowed the creative seed to flourish. By their choosing to fear less and love more, all of our lives are blessed.

I invite you to move from the pain of staying in fear and escape the mental, emotional, spiritual, and physical bonds you create from denying your intuition. Open yourself up to all possibilities, let go of expectations, remove your belief filters, and allow the process to occur. When you do, you will enter the flow of life, manifest your soul's higher purpose, and most important, embrace *Sacred Healing*.

About
Marilyn Schwader

As a Writing and Life Coach, Marilyn uses humor, compassion, and a strong sense of a writer's abilities to support and motivate her clients to become published authors. She has found that her purpose in life is to give a voice to subjects that benefit others. Her mission is to provide truthful, clear, and motivating information to those who passionately desire more in their lives. Her vision is to use her two passions—coaching and storytelling—to convey this information to as many people as possible.

Marilyn graduated from Oregon State University in Corvallis, Oregon with a Bachelor of Science degree in Technical Journalism with emphasis in Business Management. After working for several years as a technical writer contracting to high tech companies in the United States and Pacific Rim countries, she veered from the writing path and started her first business, M's Tea & Coffee House, in Corvallis.

Five years and numerous disastrous business mistakes later, she left the restaurant business and a short time later discovered Coaching. In 1998 she enrolled in Coach University and started Clarity of Vision, a Business and Life Coaching practice. The law of attraction soon worked its magic, and her talents and experience in writing soon began drawing writing clients to her business.

During this time, Marilyn undertook a three-year project to compile and publish a book about her mother's family history. From that experience, she began helping people self-publish their books. Looking for a way to combine her coaching and writing experience, Marilyn decided to create a book series that would be written by coaches and that highlighted principles and ideas supported in the coaching process.

Thus, the *A Guide to Getting It* book series was born. *A Guide to Getting It: Sacred Healing* is the sixth book in the series. The first five books are:

A Guide to Getting It: Self-Esteem

A Guide to Getting It: Achieving Abundance

A Guide to Getting It: Remarkable Management Skills

A Guide to Getting It: A Clear, Compelling Vision

A Guide to Getting It: Powerful Leadership Skills

For more information about Clarity of Vision Publishing, visit www.ClarityOfVision.com. To find out more about the *A Guide to Getting It* book series, visit www.AGuideToGettingIt.com.

To contact Marilyn, call (503) 460-0014 or email Marilyn@ClarityOfVision.com

Loving Ourselves, Living Our Lives, Healing the World

By Laura Biering

Before I get down to the business of how to heal the world, I'd like to get a couple of things straight. First of all, when I agreed to write a chapter for this book, its working title was *A Guide to Getting It: Health and Wellness*. Certainly, I felt I had a few things to offer in that category. Who doesn't, right? Then, word came that the title had change to *A Guide to Getting It: Sacred Healing*. Whoa. A little more daunting, wouldn't you say? I mean, *A Guide To Getting It: Sacred Healing* sounds like the name of a book I would buy, not one in which I would be appearing as a contributing author! But I committed, so here I am.

And now, for the second thing that I want to make clear. Every single idea, assertion, and conclusion that I'm about to present, I came to believe as a result of my own experience and is all absolutely true—*for me*. You see, I don't want you thinking that I think of myself as some kind of guru who has all of the answers. Because I'm not—and I don't. I do believe, however, that somewhere deep inside, I have all of the answers for me, and I believe that to be true for you as well. So I simply want to be a part of your process as you discover and claim those answers for yourself. Think of me as someone who has had a lot of experiences, and who has learned a thing or two from some of them (much like you have, I am sure). I offer my learning to you, in the hope that it assists you in finding—not *my* way—but *your* own way. If the information and insights in this chapter serve as an affirmation of the path you are on, a confirmation of the way you *don't* want to go, or if you take some of what I say and leave the rest, I will be pleased that I forged ahead with my commitment (instead of running from it—and fast). To reiterate, I am not your authority figure. You are. And to help me make this point, I'd like to quote an actual guru, the Buddha, who said, "Believe nothing, no matter where you read it, or who has said it, not even if I have said it, unless it agrees with your own reason and your own common sense."

Okay, now we can start.

What exactly is this thing called *Sacred Healing*? When looking up the word "sacred" in the dictionary, the definitions I liked the best were the ones that said "entitled to reverence and respect" and "highly valued and important." These definitions also included the word holy, so I looked that up, too—as well as the words heal, healthy, and whole. Not surprisingly, I learned some interesting things. So as not to turn this into an etymology lesson, however, let me just say that each of those words was inextricably linked to the others. The definitions included words such as intact, well, and restored, as well as unbroken, perfect, divine, and sacred! Hmm…

You may be saying to yourself at this point, "Yeah, yeah, I know. This is all very interesting (or not), but what does this have to do with how we heal the world by loving ourselves?" Okay. This information doesn't readily answer that big question for me, either. It does, however, begin to shine some light on another question I have been asking for some time, which will lead us into the topic of the chapter, I promise: How am I to reconcile my need for healing *and* the fact that I am perfect at the same time? I mean, aren't we *all* in need of some kind of healing? And aren't we *all*, at the same time, whole and perfect just as we are? And isn't the same true for our *world*?

I have been in need of healing a number of times in my life—from traumatic childhood experiences, a life-threatening eating disorder, and a career-ending creative block, to name a few. And I now know that none of that means that there is anything wrong with me. I ask you, if there were a scratch or a clump of mud on the ceiling of the Sistine Chapel, would it be any less a masterpiece? No! I propose that the same is true for us. And this is what came to me as a result of the dictionary search: There is *human* healing, with which we all have some experience, and then there is *Sacred Healing*.

In *Walking in this World*, her sequel to the classic, *The Artist's Way*, Julia Cameron addresses the *Sacred Healing* issue beautifully. She suggests that we are in need of healing not because we are sick. What is in need of healing is "the rift between our spiritual stature and our mistaken perception of ourselves as flawed." When I read that, it stopped me in my tracks—it still does. Of course—that's *Sacred Healing*! So how do we get it—for our world and ourselves?

I believe that our world is like a puzzle and that each of us has a space to fill within that puzzle, a space that's ours and ours alone. Therefore, I believe that we must do what it takes to fill that space, because nobody else can, or will. It seems to me that the only way to fill our space is by doing what we're created to do, *which is to be ourselves*. And it is only by being ourselves that we, as individuals, have a chance for rich, fulfilling lives, and that the world has a chance to function at its optimum level, which is a state of peace. And don't we all want that?

So being yourself—saying what you think, doing what you feel called to do, following your dreams—is not only your right, but also your responsibility!

Now "being ourselves" sounds so simple, when in actuality it can be quite a challenge. This is especially true when we have spent much of our lives trying to live by external standards. One of my favorite poets, e. e. cummings, said, "To be nobody but yourself in a world which is doing its best, night and day, to make you everybody else, means to fight the hardest battle that any human being can fight." At first reading of this quote, I was right there with him, and I am still with him in the spirit of the words. But, as I thought more about it, I realized there was one thing harder for me than trying to be myself: Trying to be someone else! Think about it. How much more energy does it take to live up to other people's expectations, to hold back our brilliance, and to play small when we are really huge—of spiritual stature, no less?

You may have heard that the great Michelangelo said that he didn't carve his masterpiece, The David, out of the rock. He said that, instead, he simply chipped away what wasn't David, until only David remained. Cool, huh? This is what I am suggesting we do. We must see ourselves as the beautiful, magnificent, divine creatures that we are, and, at the same time, let go of anything that isn't in alignment with that. In essence, we chip away what isn't ourselves, until only we remain. I know, I know—simple, but not easy! Perhaps. But whether or not you know what the reason is for you to be here, there is one. Richard Bach suggests that if you want to find out whether or not your mission on Earth is finished, try this test: "If you're alive, it isn't."

So I am assuming that since you are reading this, you are alive, and there is still work for you to do in this world. And as daunting as that may seem, it doesn't have to be. The outline of the process I am suggesting follows this paragraph. It appears to be linear, doesn't it? And, for the purposes of the outline, it is. In reality, however, it is linear, iterative, and holographic all at the same time! It's a cycle, a spiral, a ripple effect, a positive snowball, if you will! It *does* happen in order, we *do* visit the same topics over and over with new insights and information, *and* as we are involved in our individual processes, each individual thought, choice, and action is having an impact on the world! Whew! If I have lost you here, bear with me. My hope is that this will come clear as we look at each item in the outline in more detail. The outline:

Loving Ourselves
- Recognizing (the rift)
- Claiming (our divinity)

- Accepting (our humanity)
- Discovering (our authenticity)

Living Our Lives
- Choosing and acting (consciously and lovingly)
- Expressing (fully)
- Leading (others)

Healing the World
- Co-creating with others and the Great Divine

Loving Yourself: Recognizing the Rift

As you can see, *Sacred Healing* begins with individual healing, which begins with loving yourself. First of all, we must recognize the need. My guess is that you wouldn't have picked up this book if *Sacred Healing* weren't a concern of yours, on some level. So, what about your life do you feel needs healing?

- Are you destructive, engaging in unhealthy behaviors, such as habits or addictions, or remaining in unhealthy relationships or job situations?
- Do you have no sense of purpose for your life, no concept of your mission for your time here on Earth?
- Are you experiencing very little joy or fulfillment, and wondering if this is all there is?
- Are there things in your life that simply aren't working as you would like, and other things that are working, but that you would like to be experiencing more smoothly or fully?
- Would you like to be happier when you get up in the morning and start your day?
- Has it been a while since the last time you sat still and listened to your inner wisdom?
- Do you have a hard time doing what you say you want to do?

If so, I would venture to say that you are in need of *Sacred Healing*. Of course, only you know if this is true for you. Do you see yourself as insignificant, broken, or flawed? Or have you claimed your spiritual stature?

Claiming your Divinity

After we recognize that there is a need for *Sacred Healing*, the next step is apparent. It is to claim that which is true about us. By this I mean our magnificence, our creativity, our complexity—our divinity. It is to remember, or to know for the first time, our spiritual stature, and to acknowledge and embody it as a fact of life, both figuratively and quite literally, too!

Just as the whole "Loving... Living... Healing" process isn't linear, neither is claiming your spiritual stature. It isn't that way for me, anyway. It is something I have to remind myself of over and over and over again. It is something I must consciously choose to claim, certainly on a daily basis, and often moment by moment. My hope is that for all of us, it will become easier, and we will soon be treating others and ourselves accordingly all the time.

Accepting your Humanity

So now that you recognize that you are divine, and you are on the path of consciously claiming that for yourself, I suggest that you also accept your humanity. I know this sounds contradictory. But stick with me. The concepts are actually complementary. The idea is that it is only by accepting your past, including your mistakes and the mistakes of others, that you can truly be in the present and move toward the future of your dreams. I am suggesting that you accept and eventually love yourself in your totality, the light and the darkness, including what has gone before and what is true now. The reality of your life so far is your starting point from which you begin to live the rest of your life. Yes, your past is your past, and it may not have been all that pleasant, but it is *not* your potential!

Here are a few tools that have helped my clients and me to shift perspectives about the past. They are: **In the past...**, **Evidence**, and **The Good Wolf**. The first is more completely known as **In the past... Today I choose....** I use this when I hear or feel myself using my past against me, or as "proof" that some circumstance or I will always be a certain way. For example, I have said to myself, "You are so lazy. You never clean the house, and you are a bad wife because of it." Well, this voice is certainly mean, and a liar, too! But for the sake of this example, let's say that there have been times when I was lazy and didn't clean when I said I would. Instead of addressing myself the mean way, which feels terrible and dooms me to always being that way, I say, "In the past, I have chosen not to clean and felt badly about it later. Today I choose to honor my commitment." See how it acknowledges what may have been true in the past, and yet frees me to make a different choice in the present?

The next tool I simply call **Evidence**. This one is based on the fact that there is evidence for whatever we want to find in this world. If you want to find evidence that yesterday your day was horrible, I'll bet you can find it, and the same is true for looking for evidence of the opposite kind. For instance, at the beginning of this year, I decided that it would be the best year yet, and began looking for evidence of that fact. And do you know that I found it— and am continuing to find it—every single day? Go ahead and try that on your past. Use it on yesterday, last year, and your childhood, too, and see if you can't find something positive with which to change your perspective.

The third tool I mentioned is similar to the last. I call it **The Good Wolf**. It is based on a wonderful Cherokee legend I found on the Internet. (If you know any more about the origin of it, please let me know.) It is about a grandfather who was teaching his grandson about life. "A fight is going on inside of me," the grandfather said to the boy. "It is a terrible fight and it is between two wolves. One of the wolves is evil. He is anger, envy, sorrow, regret, greed, arrogance, self-pity, guilt, resentment, inferiority, lies, false pride, superiority, and ego. The other wolf is good. He is joy, peace, love, hope, serenity, humility, kindness, benevolence, forgiveness, empathy, generosity, truth, compassion, and faith. This same fight is going on inside of you, and inside of every other person, too." The grandson thought about it for a moment and then asked his grandfather, "Which wolf will win?" The old man simply replied, "The one you feed."

Wise words, wouldn't you say? I am sure you can see how this relates to the tool of **Evidence**. Both wolves are there. We are not denying the existence of either. We are simply focusing on the good wolf, feeding it, so that it will stick around and perhaps even attract other good wolves.

Discovering your Individuality

After accepting both your divinity and humanity, what follows is finding out what makes you unique. Remember, each of us has a particular thing (or things) to offer to the world that no one else can offer. Martha Graham put it beautifully when she said, "There is a vitality, a life force, an energy; a quickening that is translated through you into action. And because there is only one of you in all of time, this expression is unique, and if you block it, it will never exist through any other medium and it will be lost. The world will not have it. It is not your business to determine how good it is, nor how valuable, nor how it compares with other expressions. It is your business to keep it yours, clearly and directly, to keep the channel open. Whether you choose to take an art class, keep a journal, record your dreams, dance your story, or live each day from your own creative source … above all else, keep the channel open!"

A little aside here: You know that this means that the next time someone says to you, "Who do you think you are, God's gift to the world?" you get to say, in all seriousness, "Why yes, I am—and so are you!" What a pleasing perspective shift it was for me when I realized that instead of being "*only* me," I am "*the* only me!"

Okay, back to the task at hand. There are so many different, wonderful, and diverse ways for any one person to begin to delve into discovering her or his authenticity. Rather than attempting a comprehensive list here, I thought I would list some of the things that I have used, and that have had a positive impact on my process. They are:

- Affirmations
- Being in community with like-minded others
- Coaching
- Conscious language
- Following a healthy food plan
- Meditation
- Network Chiropractic
- Painting, drawing, and coloring
- Offering to others what I am practicing myself
- Regular movement of my body, including yoga and expressive dance
- The 12 Steps and The 16 Steps
- The Artist's Way
- The study of Divine Feminine Spirituality
- Therapy
- Various journaling exercises
- Visualization
- Writing and reading poetry and other inspirational literature

While each of these either worked well for me along the way or is continuing to work for me, remember that I am not suggesting that if you follow this formula, that the same will be true for you. I found out that these worked for me partly by trial and error, but mostly by listening to my inner wisdom, and acting on what I heard. Let's talk for a moment about the listening part. When do you listen, and what exactly do you listen for?

You train yourself to listen all of the time (again, a process). You listen when you are sitting peacefully, when you are running errands, when you are at work, when you are making love. You work toward being in contact with your inner wisdom at all times. And you listen for what's true for you in every moment. This means you listen for your values, your dreams, to your irritations, and your passions. You watch for when you are most alive and ask yourself why. Be patient with yourself, and loving. Remove the words "should" and "but" from your vocabulary, replacing them with "could" and "and." If you need to discuss what you are experiencing, by all means do so, with your spouse, a friend, your coach, therapist, or minister. But make sure that this person is supportive and wants the best for you. If, at any point you sense that this is not the case, listen to that, and stop sharing.

Look for another way to explore and let your dreams flourish. They are divining rods pointing you in the direction in which you are most likely to be in alignment with your divinity. And as you become more and more clear about your values, you will realize that they are signposts to observe and follow in the direction of those dreams.

I used to believe that we were given dreams as a cruel joke. As I was growing up I dreamed of being a lot of things in my life, but there was only one thing I had ever really wanted and had the ability to do, and yet, somehow, I couldn't make it happen for myself. When I took the time to look within, to appreciate what I had, and dream even bigger, I realized I did indeed have more than one dream. And the dreams I had were for the fulfillment of values, not the actual outcomes I had imagined! It was then that I could get back on the road toward them, with a renewed sense of commitment and hope!

Living your Life:
Choosing and Acting Consciously and Lovingly

As a result of seeing that we are divine and claiming that for ourselves, as well as our humanity, and doing the work (and play!) of discovering our authenticity, we can't help but become more and more clear about what we want and why we are here. We are listening to the wisdom we hold in our brains and in our hearts and bodies as well. This leads us to making conscious, loving choices, moment by moment, based on our values and our truest desires and dreams. We act from a belief in possibility, not based on fear or memories of the past. In short, we evolve. As we continue to listen to the wisdom within, we will be led to take further action in the direction of our dreams. We truly do co-create our lives, by thought, word, and deed. We might as well create them by design, rather than by default, right?

As we move forward, acting on what we know, feel, and want, we get clearer as we go. Sometimes there will be forks in the road; values will feel in conflict, and we will feel fear. I am not saying this will be easy for any of us. Dreams do change, and we are left with a lot of questions. Why didn't they come true? Why did I want them to? Were they really my dreams or someone else's? As I mentioned before, when I gave myself the time and space to explore these questions, some interesting answers emerged. I had been attached to the way I thought my dreams would come true. For instance, at some point in my life, I have wanted to be each of the following: teacher, nurse, actress, pop singer, torch singer, country singer, opera singer, stage director, minister, bartender, lobbyist, poet, painter, dancer, facilitator, coach, speaker, writer, wife, home owner, and a financially independent philanthropist. Some of these things I have actually achieved on some level, and for that I am grateful. However, what I am even more grateful for, is the fact that I now know why I wanted those things. I wanted them because of my values, specifically the following:

- Connecting with others by listening and being heard
- Loving and being loved as unconditionally as is humanly possible
- Having an impact on the lives of others by educating, entertaining, inspiring, enlightening, and empowering them
- Earning a degree of financial security so that I can be comfortable and assist others
- Experiencing the full range of self-expression

I have now freed myself to see the evidence that I am living my values. Also, because they are not tied to certain outcomes, I get to choose to honor them on a more consistent basis.

By loving ourselves exactly as we are, we begin to better know ourselves, and become more and more open to possibilities and choices. There was a time I didn't believe I had choices, and so I was bound by that belief. In effect, as long as I believed that, I was right, at least about conscious choices. But I am here to say that we always have choices, even if it is about how we will see and react to a situation. Viktor Frankl said, "We who lived in concentration camps can remember the men who walked through the huts comforting others, giving away their last piece of bread. They may have been few in number, but they offer sufficient proof that everything can be taken from a man but one thing: the last of the human freedoms—to choose one's attitude in any given set of circumstances, to choose one's own way."

Expressing Fully and Authentically

Still with me? Okay! Now that we know and accept ourselves, and consciously love ourselves with thought, word, choice, and action, we are expressing ourselves fully and authentically. We are courageous and take risks, in service of others and ourselves. And in our vulnerability we have access to more personal power than we ever thought possible.

Leading Others

This is where the snowball effect I mentioned earlier really begins to be seen. We move out of the realm of loving only ourselves and into loving others by leading them. Certainly there are instances where we lead formally, either large groups of people or one-on-one. Even more often than that, however, we are leading informally, indirectly, by being an example. We are modeling for others and giving permission to them to do the same. I am sure you know the Marianne Williamson quote that Nelson Mandela used in his 1994 Inaugural Speech. I repeat it here to reiterate their point:

Our deepest fear is not that we are inadequate.
Our deepest fear is that we are powerful beyond measure.
It is our light, not our darkness that most frightens us.
We ask ourselves, 'Who am I to be brilliant, gorgeous, talented, and fabulous?'
Actually, who are we not to be?
You are a child of God.
Your playing small doesn't serve the world.
There's nothing enlightened about shrinking so that other people won't feel insecure around you.
We were born to make manifest the Glory of God that is within us.
It's not just in some of us: it's in everyone.
And as we let our own light shine, we unconsciously give other people permission to do the same.
As we are liberated from our own fear, our presence automatically liberates others.

Healing the World

Can you see how recognizing "the rift between our spiritual stature and our mistaken perception of ourselves as flawed," claiming our divinity, accepting our humanity, discovering our authenticity, choosing and acting consciously and lovingly, expressing ourselves authentically and fully, and leading others to do the same, can instantly begin the process of, and ultimately lead to, the healing of the world? Just think what it will be like when we are each and every one of us being who we were created to be, filling our spaces in the universe! We will all be consciously co-creating, each of us by ourselves and with each other, and all of us with the Great Divine!

So that's my story, and I'm sticking to it, as they say. You can call me an idealist, a Pollyanna, or someone in rose-colored glasses. I can't help but be excited about all of the possibilities—children growing up in a healthier and more loving world, no need for prisons or homeless shelters, people smiling and laughing and loving and living and healing all at the same time. What are the possibilities that come to your mind?

Another, simpler way that I sometimes think of this process is with the old slogan for the ecological movement: Think Globally, Act Locally. If I love myself, I can have a global impact. Now how *cool* is that?

Thank you for reading my chapter. I hope that you have felt it was time well spent. Please feel free to contact me to discuss or work on any of the topics covered. Not only would I enjoy that, but it would also give me the opportunity to honor many of my values and be myself!

Here's one more thing for you to ponder, a poem from the 14th-Century Persian poet, Hafiz:

> *Now is the time to know*
> *That all you do is sacred.*
> *Now, why not consider*
> *A lasting truce with yourself and the Divine?*

About
Laura Biering

Laura Biering is a Certified Professional Co-Active Coach and Artist's Way at Work Facilitator, holding Bachelor's and Master's Degrees in Music from Rice University. She is the Founder of True Voices, Inc., as well as the Co-Founder of Corner Office Coaching. Laura is an Ordained Minister, an active member of the International Coach Federation, the Georgia Coach Association, the Eating Disorders Information Network, and on the Advisory Board of Thrive Atlanta. Laura serves as Co-Chair of the ProWIN Professional Coaching Committee, and is a Premier Coach for eWomen Network.

Laura coaches individuals and groups, and leads classes, workshops, and retreats on subjects such as creativity, spirituality, healthy body image, and authenticity in the workplace. She is the creator of the powerful Love Your Body, Live Your Life™ programs and products. In addition to her skills and credentials, Laura brings deep levels of compassion and dedication to her work. This is due, in part, to overcoming her own personal challenges.

Prior to being a coach, Laura was an opera singer/actress and an in-house legal recruiter. Her uniquely blended background of professional and personal experiences makes her particularly suited to meet her clients where they are, and to take them where they want to go!

To contact Laura, call 404.296.8221, email at laura@truevoices.net or laura@cornerofficecoaching.com, or visit www.truevoices.net or www.cornerofficecoaching.com.

State of Mind/Body Answers

By Pam Hillinger

Not long ago, maintaining a healthy lifestyle meant eating right, exercising, and checking in yearly with your doctor ... end of story! Today, researchers are finding that our health is not only affected by what we do physically, but is also affected by how we think and feel, that is, our state of mind. In fact, there is a relatively new and growing branch of medicine called Psychoneuroimmunology (PNI), devoted to the study of interactions between the mind; the immune system; and the progression, management, and prevention of disease. The connections between state of mind, self-care, and health are so strong that they can interact in a mutually reinforcing way. I call this the *State Of Mind-Body Answers (SOMBA) Cycle*, a virtuous cycle (see definition below) where state of mind initiates self-care actions that create healthy responses (body answers). This process creates momentum for further cycles of self-reinforcing actions and results.

> ***virtuous cycle*** *One good thing leads to another. That is, a situation in which improvement in one element of a chain of circumstances leads to improvement in another element, which then leads to further improvement in the original element, and so on. (Paul McFedries www.wordspy.com)*

Norman Cousins

To illustrate this, let's look at the life of Norman Cousins, the famous Saturday Review editor and author of the book *Anatomy of an Illness*. In 1964, when he was 49, Cousins contracted a painful and degenerative disease called Ankylosing Spondylitis. His doctors gave him only three months to live. Cousins, who had read research that had linked stress to health, chose not to follow the recommended chemotherapy and radiation treatment regiment. Instead, he developed and implemented his own self-care plan, which included taking Vitamin C and incorporating some serious (pun intended) laughing sessions into his life. He spent much of his time watching hilarious movies such as Three Stooges and Marx Brothers comedies. Cousins soon required less medication and could sleep without pain. His doctors noted an unexplained decrease in inflammation. After three months, his disease was in complete remission. Cousins later became a professor at the UCLA School of Medicine, where he founded a task force to do research on the effects of laughter on health. He lived for a full 26 years after his initial diagnosis.

What was it that caused Cousins' disease to go into remission? Maybe it was just a spontaneous recovery, but research has shown that laughter is therapeutic in two ways. First, laughter decreases the stress hormone cortisol. Elevated levels of cortisol have been shown to cause high blood sugar and suppress immune activity. Second, laughter increases Immunoglobulin A (IgA) levels.[1] A study done by Herbert Lefcourt, Ph.D. at the University of Waterloo in Canada showed that IgA levels increased in research candidates after watching 30 minutes of a Bill Cosby video. As for Norman Cousins, I believe that he created his own SOMBA cycle by using his *state of mind* to implement a unique *self-care* plan that he knew would work for him. His *body answered* with decreased inflammation. He increased momentum by continuing his self-care plan. As a result, he felt even better, and eventually enjoyed a full remission.

---

[1]Immunoglobulin A (IgA) is a microbe-fighting antibody found in blood and bodily fluids such as saliva and tears. Elevated levels represent a healthy immune status or the body's ability to ward off disease.

The SOMBA Cycle

The SOMBA (State Of Mind/Body Answers) Cycle can be illustrated as a three-sided cone (see figure below).

The sides represent:

• State of Mind

• Self-Care Actions

• Body Answers (Results)

The starting point is the bottom of the cone, which depicts the beginning of a desired change. The cone widens to represent the increase in momentum or energy that occurs as your state of mind, self-care actions, and body answers build on each other to eventually create what you want. It can be likened to a tornado propelling energy upward and lifting everything in its path.

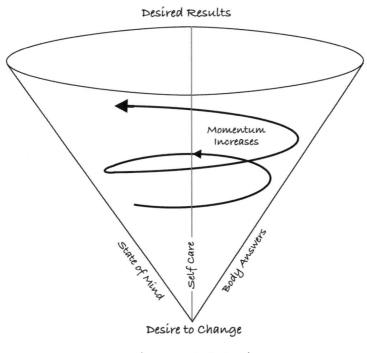

The SOMBA Cycle

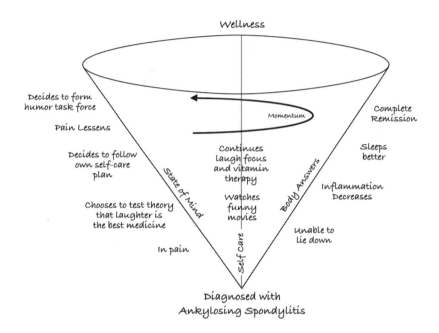

The SOMBA Cycle Applied to Norman Cousins

State of Mind

The SOMBA cycle starts with your **state of mind**, which is the first side of the cone. This represents your awareness, thoughts, emotions, beliefs, and your general outlook on life. Take, for example, optimism versus pessimism. Dr. Martin Seligman, the author of the book *Learned Optimism*, and Leslie Kamen-Siegel, Ph.D., found that optimists had higher proportions of helper T cells[2] in their blood system than did pessimists. Since this ratio is also an indication of immunity health, it stands to reason that optimists will tend to live healthier lives.

An example of how the state of mind affects self-care and your health is that of my good (and very optimistic) friend Julie. In a matter of a few years she experienced both the death of her teenage son in a tragic car accident, and a

---

[2] Helper T-cells are responsible for signaling other cells to release antibodies in the presence of a foreign substance (such as a bacteria or virus) in the body.

bout with breast cancer. I was with her when the doctors told her she had only a 50/50 chance of surviving, but heard one of the interns later say she'd do better than the average because he could tell she was an optimistic person. Julie hung in there, bravely implementing her self-care plan that included, in addition to the usual chemotherapy and radiation treatments, positive thinking, exercise, and a great deal of social interactions with supportive friends and family. One day while shopping with me, she laughingly removed her hat, exposing her bald head and announced, "Hey, everyone I've got cancer and I'm going to beat this thing!"

Julie's body answered with a full recovery. Today she is employed in a job she loves, and is managing a fund-raising event named after her son that supports scholarships for students in need. I can still hear her upbeat voice at her last birthday saying, "Hey, guys I'm doing great. I just turned 29 again!"

Self-Care Actions

"WHAT WE PLANT IN THE SOIL OF CONTEMPLATION, WE SHALL REAP IN THE HARVEST OF ACTION." ~ MEISTER ECKHART

The second step in the process, represented by the second side of the cone, is **self-care**. Self-care includes those actions that create desired change. Generally, self-care starts with taking responsibility for your own life and seriously prioritizing *you*! It means taking action to create what you want.

A study by Dr. Fawzy I. Fawzy of the UCLA School of Medicine demonstrated the value of self-care for patients with a potentially fatal cancer called malignant melanoma. Patients who obtained the most information about their disease, received assistance with coping skills and stress management, and had the most social support (all of which are self-care actions) were less likely to have the disease recur than those patients who did not receive such help.

There are many ways to practice self-care, and they are unique to each individual. They may be as simple as listening to music, reading a book, or petting a dog, or as complex as dealing with a challenging relationship, creating financial health, quitting an addiction, or treating a disease. The bottom line is that self-care includes those actions that make your life better, more joyful, and therefore healthier.

How the Body Answers

The third side of the cone, called **body answers**, is the physical response to self-care. The earliest positive physical results occur at the chemical or cellular level before we actually can see the physical changes in our body. These early responses, such as improved IgA levels, can now be measured to provide researchers with data to evaluate the effectiveness of many self-care actions.

Although problems such as high stress and depression can actually weaken our immune defenses and predispose us to diseases, positive behaviors such as laughter, expressing emotion, listening to music, and interacting with a pet can have health benefits.

Results of Self-Care Research

Self-care actions may not by themselves cure an affliction, but an increasing body of scientific evidence is documenting significant health improvement from self-care actions taken in concert with other therapies. The following are a few documented findings as to how the body answers to some specific self-care actions:

- **Humor:** Laughter has been shown to decrease the stress hormone cortisol that has been associated with high blood sugar and suppressed immune activity. Dr. Herbert Lefcourt, a psychologist at University of Waterloo in Canada, found that people with a sense of humor showed increases in IgA levels after watching Bill Cosby videos. Just as we saw with

Norman Cousins, IgA levels and defense against disease can improve with whatever happens to tickle your funny bone.

- **Social Support:** Social Support enhances health in a variety of ways. Lisa Berkman, Ph.D., of the University of California – Berkeley, conducted a study of over 7,000 men and women and found that the presence of a strong social support network can be linked to prolonged survival in the face of diseases such as heart disease and cancer. Not only was the quantity of support important, but the quality of support also seemed to be beneficial.

- **Pets:** Pets are linked to improvements in the health and survival of patients with heart disease. Animal companionship can reduce blood pressure, pulse, and respiratory rates among both children and adults. A 1991 Australian study not only revealed decreases in blood pressure, but decreases in triglycerides and cholesterol among pet owners. For 10 months, researchers at the University of Cambridge in England tracked 71 people who had recently acquired a dog and found they enjoyed better psychological and physical health over the term of the study than those who did not own pets. The study also evaluated the effect of cat ownership and found similar, but less prolonged, results.

- **Spirituality:** Few conventional studies have been done on the effects of spirituality and health because spirituality is difficult to define and objectively measure. Nevertheless, the subject is of increasing interest. Linda Powell, an epidemiologist at Rush University Medical Center in Chicago, reviewed approximately 150 scientific research papers that attempted to establish a relationship between spirituality and health. She found one thing to be true: Those who regularly attend a spiritual service have a 25 percent decrease in mortality. My guess is that the ritual of attending a spiritual service—no matter what your religion or spiritual practice—has health benefits if you *perceive* the experience to be positive.

- **Music:** Music has been linked to increased Immunoglobulin A (IgA) levels. Researchers Carl Charnetski and Francis Brennan, in their book *Feeling Good is Good for You,* noted that "...mere exposure to resonant vibrations in the air influences [IgA levels], one of the most important chemicals in the immune system." If the music you listen to helps you to "whistle a happy tune," then it will most likely have positive effects on your health.

- **Expression:** Expression of emotions has beneficial effects. Studies by James Pennebaker, Ph.D., at the University of Texas and Roger Booth, Ph.D., at the University of Auckland (New Zealand) demonstrated that expressing any kind of emotion, even writing about it (journaling), accelerates immune activity. Repressing emotions, on the other hand, was shown to cause an immune system decline.

- **Experience Pleasure:** A 1999 study at the University of Hull in the United Kingdom provides insight into the effect of pleasure on the immune system. Participants were asked to list their most pleasurable activities and rate them in terms of pleasure or guilt. IgA levels were highest among the participants listing the greatest number of pleasures. Conversely, participants listing a large number of activities with a "guilty" rating had significantly lower than average IgA levels.

- **Love and Intimacy:** Research studies have identified a variety of benefits linked to love, sexual intimacy and health. Benefits identified have included increased IgA levels from moderate sexual activity (defined as having sex 1-2 times per week) (Charnetsky and Brennan). Barry Komisaruk, Ph.D., a neuroscientist of Rutgers University, notes: "We need love and physical intimacy to prevent illness." More recently, the January, 2004 issue of <u>Time</u> magazine included a feature article about sexual healing citing studies that have linked lower incidences of breast cancer in women and prostate cancer in men for those who were more sexually active. While the cause and effect factors are still being studied and debated, it appears that moderate sexual intimacy between loving and committed individuals can be immunologically beneficial.

Working Together Synergistically

Years ago, I witnessed a good example of how multiple self-care actions such as incorporating social support, spirit, laughter, etc. (along with the traditional medical therapies) can have powerful and positive health implications.

Jason was a twenty-something patient whom I took care of while I worked as a Registered Nurse in the Intensive Care Unit of a major regional hospital. Jason had ruptured a lung while chopping wood. The injury led to a host of serious medical complications.

When I first met Jason he was critically ill, requiring a respirator and kidney dialysis to stay alive. He was with us for several months, courageously enduring round-the-clock breathing tube suctionings, needle pokes, and dressing changes.

The ICU staff was not optimistic about Jason's prognosis. We had seen many others just like him die after prolonged suffering. Recognizing this, we approached Jason's physician questioning the appropriateness of maintaining life support. The doctor decided to keep Jason on life support, believing that the combination of conventional medical therapies he was prescribing **and** the self-care actions of Jason and his family would help him recover.

We continued our support, as did his mother who stayed by his side constantly, praying with him, playing his favorite music on tape, and even joking with him. They held onto hope, and enlisted the support of others, including family members, friends, a social worker, and the hospital chaplain.

Much to our amazement, Jason eventually recovered completely. Several months later, a handsome young man in a suit walked up to me at the doors to the ICU smiling and holding out a box of chocolates for all of the nurses to share. It was Jason. "Thank you," he said, "for not giving up on me. Without everyone's prayers and support, I would not have survived."

Here is how the SOMBA cycle worked for Jason:

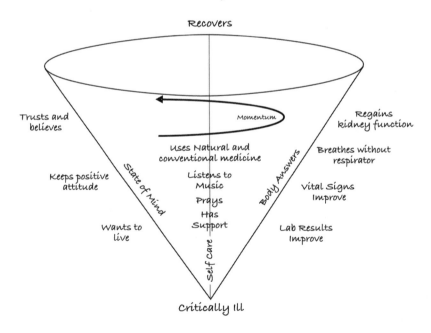

The SOMBA Cycle applied to Jason

The SOMBA Cycle **builds momentum** and becomes a virtuous cycle of self-reinforcing growth. Small steps lead to greater results, and the process continues to evolve. In reality, the progress of the SOMBA Cycle is not always steady and smooth. Some variables can speed up the process (accelerators), while others may create drag (decelerators), causing erratic progress. Examples can be seen in Susan's quest to lose weight. After losing five pounds, Susan feels lighter and more energetic. Choosing to accelerate her progress, she joins a health club and starts to consistently exercise. Now feeling really jazzed, she starts taking classes on how to prepare low fat, high-energy meals (all accelerator feelings and actions).

Unfortunately, on her way to exercise the next day, she backs her car into another car. She gets home, finds out what it will cost to get everything repaired. She feels depressed, eats a pint of ice cream, and feels fat (all decelerator feelings and actions).

Realizing that her momentum is waning, Susan chooses to reinvigorate her SOMBA Cycle by calling her coach and focusing on her progress. Feeling better, she heads back to the gym, where she learns she's lost another two pounds. As you can see, Susan is back in business. She recognized the problem (State of Mind), took action (Self-Care), and now one year later is maintaining her weight loss and is healthier because of it (Body Answers).

Implementing the SOMBA Cycle

The SOMBA Cycle teaches us that we will progress much faster if we expand our concept of self-care to include activities that enhance how we *feel*. Added to the mix of conventional medical therapies, the balanced self-care approaches of the SOMBA Cycle bring additional resources to bear, boosting us powerfully toward our goals.

Recognizing that each person's needs are unique, the following are a few general guidelines on how to practically apply the SOMBA cycle to achieve desired results.

Take a Historical Perspective

Because genetics play a strong role in your health status, it's important to learn about your family's genetic tendencies, and then research strategies to manage your specific risks. For example, if your family has a history of diabetes, make sure your self-care plan includes research on how to incorporate preventive measures such as exercise, diet, regular medical screening, and stress management. Choosing proactive self-care measures like this will make your plan far more effective than simply waiting for disease to manifest itself and then applying treatment retroactively.

Incorporate Social Support

"COMMUNITY MEANS STRENGTH THAT JOINS OUR STRENGTH TO DO THE WORK THAT NEEDS TO BE DONE. ARMS TO HOLD US WHEN WE FALTER. A CIRCLE OF HEALING. A CIRCLE OF FRIENDS. SOMEPLACE WHERE WE CAN BE FREE." ~ STARHAWK

Never underestimate the power of a strong social support network. Ascertain whether or not specific people decelerate or accelerate your SOMBA Cycle, and focus on the latter. If Uncle Wilbur's jabs about your appearance bother you, either confront him or reconsider whether it is worth being around him. Surround yourself with supportive, loving people that make you feel good. Join a club, visit family, or just throw a party. Know that doing so will enhance your health.

Get Professional Help

Most people aren't aware of what is stifling their SOMBA Cycle momentum. A good therapist or coach can help enhance your awareness, offer feedback, hold you accountable, and help you stay on track. Such professionals are committed to your agenda and can assist you in developing a customized self-care plan to overcome obstacles and achieve goals. With their unbiased perspective, they can help you see what slows your momentum in the SOMBA Cycle and can brainstorm ways to minimize your decelerators. Similarly, they can help you see what increases your momentum, and can explore ways to maximize your accelerators. A good coach or therapist sees you as the capable and powerful person that you are and will hold you accountable to be that person.

Also seek the help of other professionals that are appropriate to your unique self-care plan. Professionals such as healthcare providers, educators, financial advisors or career counselors have a wealth of information and are usually eager to share it. For example, if you want to become more financially secure as part of your self-care plan, interview a few well-recommended financial advisors (most offer free initial consultations), gather information and formulate a plan. Just remember to be bold, ask questions and tell them exactly what you want.

Laugh

As we saw with Norman Cousins, laughter can have dramatic influence on well being. A good belly laugh now and then makes us more resilient to the stresses of life and helps us put our challenges into perspective. Laughter is a gift to yourself and, when shared with others, is a gift to them too. Rent a comedy video, watch reruns of *Candid Camera, Friends, Seinfeld, Fraser, Saturday Night Live,* subscribe to *Comedy Central,* read the funnies, subscribe to comedy web site newsletters, hang out with funny friends or family members, or even take a class on how to do stand up comedy yourself. By allowing yourself to indulge in whatever you find funny, you will improve your defense against disease.

Spend Time with a Pet

Get yourself a pet. The loyalty and unconditional love that a pet has to offer will, most likely, make you feel good *and* enhance your immune system. Remember, no matter how bad your day is, you can always count on Fido. He could care less if you've made a mistake at the office, lost your temper or had a bad hair day. He'll always be there when you come home, wagging his tail and delighted to see you...a true testimony to unconditional love.

Honor Spirit

Incorporate a consistent spiritual practice in your life, whether it is attending a church, a synagogue, prayer group or simply taking routine walks in nature. I believe that a spiritual practice enhances your sense of peace, sense of trust, and provides a means for more successfully dealing with life's stresses and traumas. Commune with your Spirit in whatever way you find comfortable, and it will bring benefits beyond measure.

Express your Feelings

"WHEN WE EXPRESS OURSELVES MORE FULLY, WE DISCOVER THE TRUE JOY OF BEING." ~ RABBI THEODORE FALCON

Don't stifle your feelings. Buy yourself a journal and consistently express them on paper. This can be therapeutic. Give yourself permission to appropriately vent your feelings to a trusted professional, friend, or family member. Expressing your feelings through other methods such as dance and art can also be helpful. Be aware, however, that feelings such as remorse, sadness, anger, and fear over an extended period of time are not healthy and should be addressed with the assistance of a qualified health care provider.

Listen to Music

Stimulate your brain with whatever music you enjoy. Attend concerts or buy a CD. With the abundance of online music stores and digital players, it is now possible to take the music wherever you go. Instead of idly sitting in traffic and listening to the news, switch to your favorite music station. Take up an instrument that interests you, and play to your heart's content. Remember, you don't have to be a Mozart to gain the health benefits. Better yet, join in a group that shares your passion and let the music begin!

Experience Pleasure

Keep in mind that pleasure can be immunologically beneficial. Find out what brings you pleasure, anticipate it, and experience it. It could be partaking in a favorite hobby, a drive through the woods, skiing with a friend, attending a party, or a romantic evening for two. Too often we solely focus on tasks we feel that we *have* to do, and forget to make time to savor the things we *love*. Include pleasurable activities in your SOMBA Cycle self-care plan, and the pleasure will be all yours!

Other Positive Self-Care Actions

To promote relaxation, enhance energy, and lessen stress and pain, consider incorporating one or more of the following self-care actions into your SOMBA Cycle:

- Creative imagery
- Physical activity, be it walking, swimming, running, dance, weight lifting, or the like; the key is to do what you enjoy and do it regularly.
- Yoga
- Hypnosis
- Massage
- Meditation
- Acupuncture
- Tai Chi
- Support groups
- Book reading
- Volunteer activities

Maintain an Optimistic Frame of Mind

Recognize the health benefits of maintaining a positive outlook. It might mean taking responsibility for your life and releasing the tendency to be negative or to judge in the form of blaming, labeling, or gossiping. Change your interior dialog to be more loving and supportive of yourself and others. Drop the "I give up" habit. Know that most of life's challenges are temporary, and aren't personal in nature. Allow yourself to be less of a perfectionist by viewing mistakes as a part of being human and an opportunity for growth and learning. Be open to all of life's possibilities and you'll gain the freedom to build a fulfilled and rewarding life.

Balance

As in any system, the SOMBA Cycle relies on balance to sustain itself. Too much of a good thing (accelerators) can overload and, in turn, decelerate the cycle. For example, having a job that you like is a good thing, but too many 12 to 14 hour workdays in a week can add up, wreak havoc with your state of mind, and have negative results on your physical health. In much the same way, a spinning top that goes too fast can spin out of control and topple over. Conversely, going too slow deprives the top of the momentum it requires to stay in motion. Monitor how you feel and how you are conducting your life. If you feel that your life is out of balance, it probably is. Ask for help, and make adjustments to maintain the balance you need to create the life you want.

Implications for Coaches

For some time the coaching profession has focused on self-care concepts, employing them to help clients achieve goals such as getting the job they want, gaining financial success, getting organized, finding peace, navigating a challenged relationship, and so on. The SOMBA cycle tells us that we need to *expand* our concept of self-care.

The SOMBA cycle incorporates more than a one-size-fits-all prescription for attaining what you want with your life. Because the SOMBA cycle recognizes state of mind, self-care actions, *and* body answers (physical results), it creates a systematic, holistic, and personalized approach in helping clients achieve even more with their lives.

In the future, coaches will be seen more as health stewards, helping to bring about not only fulfillment and joy, but also health and well being. For example, when a coach is working with a client challenged with financial issues, the coach is doing much more than enhancing the client's financial bottom line. The coach is *really* helping the client achieve a customized self-care plan that will enhance the client's state of mind and thereby benefit the client's immune system and health, in addition to the client's financial status. If the plan is continually monitored and adjusted to best suit the client's ever-changing needs, the momentum of the SOMBA Cycle will continue to build, forever enhancing their lives.

Conclusion

There are many variables that affect health. Following the SOMBA Cycle is not an absolute cure-all to health issues, and will not necessarily keep you from contracting a specific affliction. However, following the SOMBA Cycle creates momentum and builds results. For example, while petting a dog or listening to Mozart may not by themselves appear to improve your health, quite possibly the *cumulative* effects of integrating a broad range of self-care actions *along with* conventional medical therapies just might improve your odds. Just as a single candle in the darkness does not shed much light, many candles put together can brighten the darkest night. What if we were to quit smoking, lose weight, eat balanced meals, cut down on alcohol intake and consistently seek help in resolving our challenges? How would the body answer then? It is my belief that our body's answer would be enhanced immunity, improved health and a life you were meant to live.

About
Pam Hillinger

Pam Hillinger, R.N., B.S.N., C.P.C. is a graduate of the University of Washington School of Nursing. She also is a graduate of the Academy of Coach Training and is a Certified Professional Coach. Her career history includes caring for patients with both chronic and acute illnesses. Pam worked as a team leader in a Seattle area hospital intensive care and coronary surgical recovery unit. She also served as the Research Coordinator and Manager for the University of Washington's Dialysis Research center, operated under the direction of world-renowned dialysis pioneer Dr. Belding Scribner. During this period, she participated in studies of medications and procedures to enhance the quality of life for kidney dialysis patients.

Pam sees a direct relationship between how people perceive their lives and the status of their health. She believes that each person has a unique purpose and potential that must be manifested to achieve a fulfilled and happy life. Her coaching practice, therefore, focuses on clients that want to align their lives with their purpose. She works with them to assess and implement a broad range of individualized self-care actions that help them not only achieve their potential and life fulfillment, but live healthier lives in the process.

Pam has had numerous guest appearances on KKNW's "Positive Talk Radio" broadcast in the greater Seattle area. She served as the coaching segment coordinator for this radio show, which featured a variety of coaching related topics. She has also been a guest speaker for professional organizations, addressing a variety of topics including "Foundations to Success," and hosted the "Best Life Series" for a community outreach program presented by a major national book retailer. She is the owner and principal of Potentia Coaching.

Outside of nursing and coaching, Pam has served in a variety of volunteer roles creating opportunities for women to connect with others and realize their potential. She resides on Whidbey Island, Washington. To contact Pam, email her at Pam@PamHillinger.com or visit www.PamHillinger.com.

The Healing Power of Solitude

By Alexis McKenna

The Interior Landscape

Western society and culture tends to focus on the external self—those aspects of self that can be measured, catalogued, and labeled. The interior landscape—the realm of thought, feelings, impressions, yearnings, dreams, and visions—is largely ignored and discounted. This interior realm, an unknown and seldom-explored inner world, is the source of qualities we most treasure: beauty, compassion, caring, and creativity. While we spend a good deal of time learning how to analyze, understand, and communicate with our external self, we spend almost no time learning how to understand and communicate with our internal self.

This internal self communicates largely in symbols, feelings, images, random thoughts, and sensations. It is not linear. It is impressionistic, quixotic, and whimsical. It can be engaged, but not dominated. It can be encountered, but not contained. It can be explored, but not mapped. When it is approached with reverence and treated with respect, it can yield astonishing information and heal us in ways that are both profound and mysterious. Establishing avenues of communication with this vast, interior landscape can most easily begin in solitude—particularly solitude in nature.

Definitions

Solitude

Most dictionaries define solitude in words and phrases such as, "the state of being alone; loneliness, seclusion." Monastic and mystical traditions describe solitude in entirely different terms. The mystics and the monastics moved deep into silence to experience direct communication with the divine—to know the divine more fully in its many aspects. The mystics reported that in descending into silence, they experienced joy, ecstasy, rapture, healing, insight, and illumination.[1] When I talk about solitude, I am referring to it in mystical terms—solitude as welcoming, embracing, nourishing, inspiring, and illuminating.

Healing

Most people think the word healing means to "fix or cure." This is one meaning of the word. Another meaning is "to make whole or sound; to restore to health." This is closer to what I experience as healing. I don't cure or fix anything; what I do is expand the framework or context in which I perceive things so that new possibilities—solutions and resolutions—emerge. The conditions that I am dealing with have not necessarily changed. What has changed is my perception of those conditions. By shifting my perception, I am able to respond differently because I literally see things differently. When I can respond differently, then problems resolve themselves and solutions emerge; a "healing" occurs.

Solitude as Living Presence

For me, solitude is like a warm friend. It is a non-judgmental presence that enfolds me in its unconditional love; it listens patiently while I question, complain, rant, rave, cry, or feel sorry for myself. Solitude never judges; it always listens with complete attention. And when I am ready to listen, it speaks to me—through the elements, the animals, and direct knowing. Ideas, feelings, images,

---

[1] Johnston, William M., Ed. (2000). *Encyclopedia of Monasticism*. Fitzroy Dearborn Publishers; Chicago, IL; vol. 2, pp. 1173-1174.

thoughts, and insights are dropped directly into my mind. The process is effortless. I do not have to *do* anything other than be still and listen. Solitude does the rest.

Entering Solitude with an Attitude of Respect

When I enter solitude, I know that I am moving deep into the heart of consciousness, and I treat it with great respect. I recognize it as a fully functioning intelligence of great wisdom that communicates mostly in symbols, through the unfamiliar senses of warmth, light, feeling, and intuition.

I have rituals for entering solitude and rituals for exiting solitude.[2] Deliberately using ritual to enter and exit solitude is the way I send a signal to myself that I am leaving the realm of ordinary, everyday affairs and entering the realm of non-ordinary affairs. I am reminding myself that I am entering a realm that is governed by a different set of rules and a different system of logic. Performing the ritual—the ceremony of acknowledgement—also reminds me that I have a relationship with solitude. It is like a beloved friend with whom I have a close and intimate relationship. Consequently, in my interactions with it, I follow the rules of relationship: loving, giving, listening, knowing, respecting, trusting, and honoring.

By loving I mean being aware of how I interact with solitude:

- What am I bringing to the dialogue?
- What impact am I having?
- How am I behaving?
- Am I being courteous, respectful, etc?
- Do I listen without judgment?
- Do I give as well as take?

[2] The dictionary defines ritual as "an established or prescribed procedure for a religious or other rite; an observance of set forms in public worship; a ceremony."

I honor solitude by giving it my complete attention, trust, and respect. If I am going to go into solitude with a question or a concern, then I need to accept whatever I learn, discover, or experience as honest information lovingly given, whether I like it or not, whether it's an answer or a deepening of the question. I don't say to solitude, "That is not the answer I want to hear; give me another one." What I might say is, "Can you clarify that? Can you deepen my understanding of that?" I trust the information that I am given and I work with it the best that I can.

Establishing a Relationship with Solitude: Creating a Sacred Place

Let me give an example of one of the ways that I develop a relationship with solitude. I live not far from a small park that has what I've defined as a sacred place—a sacred grove. This is a place where all four mystical elements—earth, air, water, and fire—come together. The area I have defined as my sacred grove is on the far side of the park. Here, a group of ancient trees overlooks a small stream that meanders through the park. I can sit with my back against an old oak tree, face the stream, feel the wind on my cheek, and look up through the leaves to see the sun shining brightly above.

When I first found this place in the park, I asked it if it was willing to be a sacred place. I addressed each element[3] separately and told it what I wanted to do. And then I waited to hear its response. The response was not immediate; it developed over a period of time.

When I spoke to the tree, I identified it with the element of earth. I asked the tree if it was willing for me to sit at its

[3] Different mystical traditions ascribe different qualities (or characteristics) to the four elements. In my mystical training, these are the qualities that are associated to each of the elements: (1) earth = strength, grounding, steadiness, the forces of gravity, mountains; (2) air = ideas, concepts, thinking, circulation of information, breaking up of old thoughts or forms, wind; (3) fire = vitality, passion, compassion, vision, enlightenment, the sun, heat; and (4) water = emotions, feelings, cleansing, healing, love, flowing, flexible, the moon, coolness.

feet, to have me lean my back against its trunk, and to assist me in pulling energy up from the earth for the purposes of grounding, stability, and centeredness. And then I waited. I didn't do anything. I just observed my body. What I noticed is that I felt calmer, more centered, and less tense. I felt the warmth of the tree against my back and had the sense that the tree was sheltering me—holding me—in its loving embrace. I took this as a "yes."

Next I spoke to the wind (air). I asked the wind if it was willing to be a conduit of ideas and information. Was it willing to help me release old ideas and concepts and embrace new ones? Was it willing to be an agent of change and transformation? Again, I waited. The day was still. As I sat there in silence, leaning against a big oak tree that was perched on the edge of the small ravine leading down to the steam, a breeze emerged from nowhere. The leaves of the tree directly in front of me were swaying and moving even though the leaves of other trees in the park were still. I also noticed that new ideas popped into my mind. Before I came to the park that day, I had been doing some internal processing around some important relationships in my life. I was at an impasse. I'd arrived at a place where I knew I needed to change even though I didn't know precisely how to change. As I was sitting there watching the leaves sway, I suddenly had an inspiration. I began to see how I might do things differently. I had not specifically asked for this information; it just dropped into my mind. I decided that the wind was telling me—through the rustling of the tree leaves and the giving of this spontaneous insight—that it was willing to be a conduit of ideas and information.

Speaking to the water is, in some ways, the most challenging, for it moves without seeming to move at all. I asked the stream if it was willing to help me get more in touch with my own feelings, as well as to be the repository for old emotions that I wanted to release. I watched the water as it moved sluggishly around a tree that had toppled into the stream, and I waited. Gradually, I began to notice that I felt a release of emotional tension in my body. I experience emotional tension differently than I experience physical tension. Physical tension feels like static in my muscles. Emotional tension feels like a weight on my heart. When I am able to release emotional tension, I usually notice that my chest relaxes. I am breathing deeper and I feel more peaceful and calm. As I sat there watching the water, I realized that I felt more emotionally centered and nourished. The circumstances of my life had certainly not changed in those minutes. What *had* changed was my ability to cope with them. I felt more emotionally at ease and hopeful—less worn out and discouraged.

In some ways, light (fire) is the easiest element for me to work with. As I sat with my back against the tree, listening to the gentle sounds of the water and feeling the soft wind on my cheek, I looked up at the sky. I always speak directly to the sun—even when I cannot see it. I asked it if it was willing to give me strength, passion, vitality, and courage. If the answer is "yes," then I will almost immediately start feeling more energized, more optimistic, and more willing to pick myself up and do whatever needs doing. Sometimes, that internal shift in energy is actually accompanied by a shift in light: the sun actually shines through the clouds or leaves and falls on me directly. At other times, I don't see it at all; I just sense a strengthening of my own internal light—my internal fire, my internal motivation. When I respond this way, I assume that I am getting a "yes" answer from the light.

Every time I go to my sacred grove in the park, I greet the elements by name. I use their metaphysical names: good morning gnomes (earth); good morning undines (water); good morning sylphs (air); good morning salamanders (fire). I do this quite deliberately. By using a different language—a different system of designation—I force myself to be conscious of what it is that I am doing and why. Often, the elements respond directly to these greetings. The tree against which I am leaning will sway slightly, the breeze moves gently through the leaves, the water ripples and gurgles a little bit, and the sun will break through the clouds or leaves. Coincidence? Perhaps. I prefer to believe that it is a social ritual of acknowledgement and mutual respect.

When I leave my sacred grove, I name each element and I thank it for the specific gift that it has given me that day. Sometimes the gift I've received is the gift of feeling more relaxed, more centered, and calm. Sometimes the gift I've received is a specific idea or concept. And sometimes the gift I've received is a reminder not to take myself so seriously. There are times when various creatures—bugs, birds, animals—come into my line of vision and make me laugh out loud with their antics: squirrels chasing each other around the tree or cats throwing themselves down on the ground, demanding in a loud voice to be petted.

Deepening the Relationship: Active and Passive Questions

Over a long period of experimentation, I have developed the habit of working with solitude and the elements of nature in two general ways: active and passive. When I am working passively with nature and the elements, I simply go out into them and observe whatever there is to observe. When I am fully conscious, I empty my mind and just wait—knowing that sooner or later something will catch my attention. When something does catch my attention, I assume that is the beginning of a dialogue or conversation. At other times, when I am unconscious or preoccupied with my own thoughts, I am startled into consciousness and dialogue by an unusual experience or event.

Passive

One day I was out walking. I know that I was feeling somewhat discouraged—probably depressed—and definitely into some self pity. I honestly don't remember what it is that I was feeling morose about; I just remember that I was feeling that way. I was walking along a street not far from where I live, when I suddenly had my attention drawn to a telephone pole at the end of the street. I don't know what made me look up; I just know that I did. There, sitting on top of the telephone pole, was a vulture. The vulture was looking at me directly. After a few moments of this direct eye contact, the vulture took off and flew away. This was a very startling experience for me. I had never looked at a vulture "eyeball to eyeball." I knew I had better pay attention. I didn't know what this was all about, but I knew I was receiving a message of some kind.

When I finished my walk I went home and looked up "vulture" in Ted Andrews' *Animal-Speak: The Spiritual and Magical Powers of Creatures Great and Small*. The basic meaning of the vulture, according to Andrews, is "purification—death and rebirth—new vision."[4] At the time I encountered the vulture, I was struggling with my career. I was feeling uneasy and was trying to make some decisions about what direction to take in my life. I felt that my encounter with vulture was telling me that I was not thinking radically enough. I felt I had been given a clear message that there were some things that needed to die in order for others to be born. I took this notion into my journal writing time and began working with it in that form. Eventually, I sought some counseling; I wanted to more fully explore what needed to die. I had the sense that there were parts of me that I needed to release, and parts of me that I needed to embrace. I began an internal dialogue with myself that lasted many months.

Ultimately, through the journal writing, counseling, and further meditation, I concluded that it was time to make a major change in my career. Shortly after I made that

[4] Andrews, Ted (1998). *Animal-Speak: The Spiritual and Magical Powers of Creatures Great and Small*. Llewellyn Publications, St. Paul, MN., p. 200.

decision, I heard a whisper in meditation. I was directed to look in a specific newspaper in the library. I went to the library and consulted that publication, *The Chronicle of Higher Education,* and found an advertisement for a job that was exactly what I was looking for. I applied for the job and was hired. As a result of taking that job, I sold my home, moved to another state, and began a whole different line of work. Might I have done all of this without ever having met vulture? Probably. However, there is no doubt in my mind that meeting the vulture in that very direct and startling way made me pay attention. Vulture was a catalyst. I was already in the process of rumination; his appearance in my life just intensified the process and made me pursue it with more concentration and focus.

Active

When I lived in Northern California, I had the habit of going out to walk at one of the local parks that had a large lake. I'd walk around the lake, working on a particular question as I walked. One day, I was wondering if I was really on track with my soul's journey. Was I really doing what it was that my soul wanted me to do? I didn't know the answer to this question. I knew that spirituality was important to me. I had committed many resources—time, energy, and money—to the pursuit of my spirituality. I did my best to live according to my understanding of spiritual principles; and, I wasn't really sure that I was doing that. As I was "walking with" this particular question, a crane caught my attention. The crane had been down on the shore of the lake as I approached it. The bird took flight and flew directly across my line of vision in a diagonal direction. There was no way I could miss it. I felt the crane's dramatic appearance and pattern of flight—directly across my line of sight—was important. I thought it was, in some way, a response to my question.

When I went home, I looked up the meaning of the word "crane" in Circlot's *Dictionary of Symbols*. One of the meanings—taken from the Chinese—was that the crane symbolized "the good and diligent soul."[5] When I read that, tears sprang into my eyes. I realized that I had received a direct answer to my question. I *was* on track with my soul's journey; and, I wanted to know more. I found a rock with a picture of a crane painted on it. I put that rock on my altar because I wanted to start a dialogue with my soul. The rock was a visual reminder of the desire—my commitment—to communicate. In meditation, I asked my soul to teach me how to listen. I asked my soul to teach me how to communicate with it.

One day, as I sat in meditation, feeling like I had dozed off, I suddenly heard a voice inside my mind say clearly, "I have been with you through all time and all space." I started to weep. I felt such a sense of gratitude and relief. I was sure that this was my soul speaking to me, telling me that it had always been there and would always be there. I then had a series of recollections of times in my life when I had been in despair and had received information—through a friend, a conversation, a book, or film—that had given me renewed hope and inspiration. I realized that those were times when my soul had been speaking to me. I then began a series of dialogues—again through journal writing— where I asked my soul to teach me how to dialogue with it more directly before I reached those levels of despair. In essence, I was asking my soul if it would teach me how to call upon it and access its wisdom, before I got to some sort of a crisis. Over time, it taught me how to do this.

Ultimately, I learned that the easiest way for me to talk to my soul was to do a meditation I've come to call "entering the heart of darkness." When I want to communicate with my soul, I go into meditation and I imagine going into my

[5] Circlot, J.E. (1974). *A Dictionary of Symbols*. Philosophical Library, New York, NY., p. 66. Translated from the Spanish *Diccionardio De Symbolos Tradicionales*.

heart (heart chakra). From my heart, I imagine that I am connected to—literally sitting in—the heart of the universe. For me, this feels like sitting in a warm, dark, velvety place that is safe. Once I am in that safe place, I come to complete stillness and then I wait. I listen. I "feel into" the heart of the universe—into the heart of consciousness—with my unfamiliar senses—with my emotions, my intuition, and my sense of warmth. I allow myself to feel safe and loved. I express gratitude for the opportunity to sit in the heart of the universe.

From those feeling places, I listen. Sometimes I hear words and phrases. Sometimes I experience body sensations. Sometimes I cry—not because I am sad—but because the experience is beyond words. Tears of gratitude, wonder, and awe are the only "words" I have. When I return from the "heart of darkness," I feel calmer, more centered, and focused. I don't always know what it is that I have learned or experienced in the meditation. I just know that something is different. With time and concentration (in the form of meditation, journal writing, etc.) that sensation of difference will translate itself into thoughts, feelings, images, and visions that guide my actions, choices, and decisions.

Would I have learned how to do all of this if crane had not come into my life on that particular day? Probably. But again, the crane was the catalytic symbol. The crane focused my attention in a particular way. I paid attention. I looked up the meaning of the crane symbol and I began a series of dialogues with the symbol. It was out of that dialogue that I ultimately was able to discover—or create—a method of working with my soul that has allowed me to deepen my knowledge and understanding of it. I now have a better idea of the way it communicates, and what it considers important. For example, through this exploration, I first encountered the work of shamans. From those studies, I learned that shamans believe the soul is most concerned with issues of growing, learning, and meaning. When I find myself dealing with questions of meaning, I know I am in the domain of my soul. I know I am dealing with what is most important to my soul and so I seek its counsel through meditation, journal writing, and other means.

Using Other Life Events to Verify Information

The interior world is creative. It likes change, variety, and whimsy; it resists regimentation, rules, and routines. Because each of us has a unique interior world, no one can give us a "dictionary of symbols" that is exactly right for us. Symbols exist within a specific context. Each of us has to be willing to dialogue with the symbol—interact with it—and find out what its meaning is for us on that specific day. Books that suggest the possible meanings of symbols are useful. They can give us a place from which to begin our exploration. Ultimately, it's up to us to interpret the symbol(s) and give it meaning and substance (by bringing it into our life in a concrete way).

Testing our interpretation of a specific symbol is always wise. We can do this in a number of ways. We can sit down and discuss it with a close friend who is willing to listen and provide us with feedback. We can ask for verification. We can go into our inner world in meditation and ask for specific feedback. We can say something like, "If my understanding of this symbol is correct, then I'd like to receive verification. I'd like XYZ specific event to happen or I'd like other symbols to appear that confirm and clarify my understanding."

In asking for a specific event to occur, we make it "generally specific." For example, we can say, "If this symbol is telling me to explore other career options, then I'd like something in my external environment to give me the same message." This "something" can be anything from a friend who suggests career counseling, to a book falling off the shelf and opening to a specific page that provides clarification, to an article that appears in the newspaper, to an advertisement seen on television. The goal here is not to tell our inner world how to manifest. The goal is to open up a number of possibilities so that we will be paying attention. Then when the clarification or verification appears, we will notice it and respond appropriately.

Another way to get clarification is to consult a tool used for divination[6] and ask a series of questions. Tools used for divination can include stones (runes) or sticks (I-Ching) or any of the card decks (Tarot, Medicine Cards, Goddess Cards) that can be found in a metaphysical bookstore. When using a tool for divination, we usually ask a general question like, "Can you clarify the meaning of this symbol?" We then shuffle the deck, or shake up the bag of stones, and see what cards (stones) appear in response to our question. We work with each of the answers.

There are several different ways we can work with these answers. We can consult the interpretive guidebook that normally accompanies these tools. We can, for example, look up the meaning of the specific card(s) or stone(s) and then sit with it. What does it mean in this context? How does it clarify our question? How does it verify (or challenge) our understanding? Sometimes this means that we take the card or stone into meditation and see what emerges. Sometimes this means that we do journal writing about it. And sometimes it means that we place it on our personal altar and just sit with it for a period of time. There are many different ways to work with these tools. Basically, each of us must experiment until we feel that we have discovered the method that works best for us.

How do we know when the clarification or verification process is complete? Usually we know it because we get an "aha." Something clicks and we have a sense of rightness—as if all the pieces of the puzzle have fallen into

---

[6] The dictionary defines divination as "perception by intuition; attempting to discover hidden knowledge or meaning by non-ordinary methods."

place. All of us have had this experience. The feeling can be hard to describe in words, but it's quite recognizable when it happens. Most of us would say, "I just know this is it—this is the meaning for me." We then test it out by putting it into action. We make choices and decisions based on our understanding and see what kind of feedback we get from our external world. If our understanding is accurate, then things normally move along smoothly; new directions emerge and new possibilities unfold. If our understanding is inaccurate—or incomplete—things do not go as smoothly. We will experience ourselves getting off to a good start and then hitting a snag of some kind. When that happens repeatedly, we must go back to the beginning. We then ask the same question in a different way—or with more precision and detail—and see what happens. Ultimately, we will discover the meaning that is right for us.

Honing Our Skills as Explorers

Learning to work with our inner world is a skill that we develop and hone over time. In essence, we are learning to work with an entirely different communication (language) system. Learning its linguistic structures, its rules of grammar and syntax takes time. Persistence and experimentation are key. Each of us will work differently with our inner worlds. There is no one right way to do it. Teachers, classes, and books can help. They can act as catalysts by sharing their wisdom and knowledge. However, in the final analysis, we are the decision-makers; each of us decides what is best for us.

The keys to unraveling the inner symbolic world are *intention* and *attention*. If we *intend* to learn how to communicate with our inner world, then we learn to do it by paying *attention* to what is easy for us. What comes naturally to us? Where do we experience that sense of flow and ease? Where (when) do we get that sense of knowing? That's the place where we want to spend more time. A sense of ease—of flow—is basically a feedback mechanism that is saying, "You're on the right track. Spend more time here."

Reciprocating

So far, we've talked about ways that: (1) we can learn about ourselves by interacting with the mystical elements in solitude; and (2) we can interpret the information that we are given. We've focused mostly on what we can receive. Now let's look at giving. What can we give? A healthy relationship is based on mutual respect and reciprocity—each one gives something and each one gets something. So what is it that we, as human beings, are giving to nature and to the mystical elements and symbols?

- Respect: for nature's innate intelligence and wisdom.
- Recognition: seeing nature (and all of its elements) as a form of consciousness that is equal to (although different than) our own.
- Dignity: recognizing nature and those elements as autonomous. Listening with respect. Paying attention.
- Honoring: accepting the information that is given by working with it to understand and unfold its meaning (rather than discounting it by saying it has no meaning).
- Gratitude: feeling grateful for the help and the friendship.
- Humility: coming fresh to each encounter; being willing for the symbol—or the experience—to be entirely different this time.
- Playfulness: being willing to learn from play and whimsy; not valuing serious information or concepts more than playful and whimsical ones.
- Partnering: willingness to dialogue, interact, and work together in ways that can be mutually beneficial.

- Intimacy: willingness to be close, tender, and vulnerable; allowing nature (and the mystical elements) to have an impact on us; honoring and acknowledging that impact.

A Closing Wish

I hope that I have piqued your curiosity about your own rich, inner world. I hope that I've given you some ideas about how you might begin to work with solitude and the mystical elements to learn more about your self and your rich interior landscape. This inner world is a storehouse of treasures; it holds the keys to aspects of your self that will astonish, delight, and enchant you. When you approach it with reverence, respect, and a genuine desire to learn, it can heal, inspire, and transform your life in ways you cannot now imagine.

About
Alexis McKenna

Alexis McKenna, Ph.D., is a trained counselor, natural mystic, and innovative thinker who has taught at the postgraduate level. She is trained in the "hermetic" tradition of Western mysticism. It is a tradition that sees duality as an illusion that camouflages an underlying unity or wholeness: the outer world mirrors and reflects the inner world. "Once we become more conscious of the way in which we create our world, we can begin to create the world of our dreams instead of the world of our fears."

Alexis and Lynn Bieber (see chapter on "Healing Through Sound") offer a course based in Western Mysticism entitled, "Developing and Sustaining Your Personal Relationship with the Sacred." For more information call 503-838-1040 (Alexis) or 925-484-5969 (Lynn). Alexis and Lynn also offer joint readings entitled, "Infinite Possibilities."

To contact Alexis, call 503-838-1040, email amckenna@worldnet.att.net, or visit her website: www.seedingthefuture.com.

Journey Into Meditation: A Roadmap to Inner Healing and Wholeness

By Lisa Guyman

Take a breath. Notice how your breath flows. Allow it to come in and allow it to exit without any effort. Repeat. Yes, meditation starts with attention to the moment and it can be as simple and as easy as just observing your breath.

I slip into the moment so easily when I'm by the ocean. To me there is nothing more naturally meditative than listening to the ocean waves and feeling the ocean breeze. Waves go up and down endlessly, creating a soothing rhythm. Time stretches out into infinity and yet it stands still. The ocean reminds us to just be, to relax. It is in no hurry. It just is. And if we are allowed to truly be, we heal and we shine. We're expansive and limitless. But, since we all can't live by the shore, we have to bring the shore, the deeper rhythm of consciousness to us.

Meditation allows us to transcend into the ocean of our consciousness, beyond our regular thoughts and feelings and into our deep inner quiet. With meditation we switch on the light instead of analyzing the darkness. Meditation is one of the most powerful things we can do for our lives and it's not difficult to practice. In fact, it is very, very easy.

Our bodies actually have a built in self-healing mechanism that operates at its peak when we are at rest. While sleep rejuvenates us and restores us to some degree, meditation creates a unique state of profound rest, far deeper than sleep, giving our bodies the ability to heal and re-balance at the deepest level possible. When our bodies and minds are given the right conditions, the body receives healing at a fundamental level and therefore its effects show up everywhere in our lives. Meditation goes to the source and works at a causal level. This is why meditation can actually reverse the aging process.

Meditation produces benefits that far exceed the time investment. Maharishi Mahesh Yogi, the founder of Transcendental Meditation™ says, "water the root and enjoy the fruit." Why spend time treating or tending to the individual leaves or branches when what the tree needs is water and nutrients?

A meditative state seems difficult to achieve, but meditation is actually not hard, contrary to popular belief, and it doesn't require years of practice or the elimination of thoughts. Meditation is actually so simple that you can master the process in a few days. Research has even shown that individuals attending a weekend workshop on Transcendental Meditation™ exhibited a physiological state similar to Zen monks and Yoga Masters who had fifteen to twenty years of meditation experience.

There are many effective forms of meditation. There is guided meditation, walking meditation, Buddhist meditation, etc., any of which can take us on a path to deeper states of consciousness. But since my personal journey started with Transcendental Meditation™ and since TM is the most widely documented form of meditation (over 600 published studies on the state it elicits and on the benefits of meditation), it only makes sense to use TM as the jumping off point. We can also get into a meditative "zone" through art, yoga, journaling, Reiki, touch healing, acupuncture, being by the ocean, and so on. In fact, anything that allows us to be in the moment and relax deeply, both transforms and soothes us, but as I refer to meditation throughout these pages, I am referring to TM.

Commonly held myths stop people from investigating meditation and its benefits. If you have any of the following beliefs, I can see why you might not consider meditation as a practice: "Meditation is hard. It takes concentration. My mind is too busy. I can't meditate. I don't have time to meditate. I might feel peaceful during the time I practice it, but it won't affect the quality of my life. I am already happy, healthy, and pretty calm so I don't need it. It is strictly a spiritual practice so it wouldn't fit with my beliefs. It is just for people who are stressed."

What if you found out that meditation:

- is easy and natural
- lets you do less and accomplish more
- will make you happier, wiser, sharper, younger, and healthier
- surpasses anything that you presently do
- doesn't require that you believe in it (or anything for that matter) to get results

In actuality, meditation is not hard. I have to emphasize this because the belief that it is difficult is the stumbling block for many. Meditation is easy and it can be practiced anywhere, without any special postures. It is practiced by people from all walks of life, from artists to executives, from nuns to atheists, from school children to prisoners. One of the remarkable things about meditation is that people don't have to have any spiritual beliefs to practice it. People can practice the technique and get results even if they are complete skeptics and don't buy into the concept of meditation.

Meditation has been an inner refuge for me since I learned to meditate at the age of 16. And if a teenager can learn to meditate, anyone can. I was laying out by the pool on a rare sunny day in suburban Detroit when a friend and I decided "we should learn to meditate." The Yellow Pages directed us to Transcendental Meditation™ and off we went. That started my meditation journey 23 years ago. I have had "off" years, but the beauty of meditation is that it is easy to pick up again. I'm meditating again, and it feels like I'm home.

I was led back into my meditation practice by a couple of events. On a coaching survey, I was asked what message I would want to bring to the world if I had a year left to live, and meditation was my answer. I was very passionate about meditation in high school and college. In those years I inspired numerous people to take up the practice. Meditation lifts the fog out of our way and reveals our light. When our light shines more brightly, we bring more light into our lives and into the world around us. What a powerful method of healing!

Another event that returned my focus to meditation was a downshifting of my massage practice. This caused me to do some soul searching and ask what I'd really like to do on earth if I could do anything. I believe my life purpose is to help people connect to source and to support them in living an inspired, powerful, and authentic life. As a Life Coach, I work on the latter half of that equation, but I realized I wanted to give people something they could use on a daily basis and take with them on their journey of life. I've always wanted to teach meditation, but I knew teaching TM wasn't a fit for me. Then I came across Primordial Sound Meditation, PSM, a technique taught by Deepak Chopra, M.D. and I am on the road to becoming a PSM teacher. I certainly can't teach meditation if I'm not faithfully practicing it, so this jumpstarted my meditation. I'm thankful that my path has taken me back to my roots.

Meditation is different than just relaxing, sitting with eyes shut, or sleeping. Meditation evokes a specific physiological state in which the body is deep at rest and the mind is alert and yet exhibiting traits of relaxation (for example, exhibiting alpha waves). Within three minutes of meditation the body goes into a profound state of rest (far deeper than the deepest point of sleep that occurs after 4-5 hours of sleep as measured by oxygen consumption, carbon dioxide output, and metabolic rate). The meditative state is termed "restful alertness" because the practitioner is deeply relaxed, but still alert. Meditation provides the deepest rest possible, allowing the body to repair the damage of accumulated stress and heal itself at a deep level.

What I'm sharing sounds profound—it is—and yet meditations can feel quite ordinary. At times, I feel unsettled in meditation. Sometimes meditations can be quite noisy. Remember that no matter how the meditations might seem on the surface, they are effective at your core.

I meditated this morning. It wasn't anything magical, but I know it doesn't have to be. Sometimes, it feels like I'm doing nothing (that is the goal of meditation after all) because my head is filled with all the usual suspects and my body doesn't feel like it is in a very deep state of rest. I don't feel deep in these meditations; sometimes I'm even slightly frustrated. But I've learned to trust the process. The surprising thing is that those who meditate and report "restless" or "bad" meditations have been shown to evoke the same profound physiological state of "restful alertness."

I do have meditations that are quiet, still, and very peaceful, and you will too. I come out of these meditations in a deep state of being, with a feeling of total ease, slowed down in the moment. I feel more aware and present. My rushed, hectic energy gets washed away. I am quieted, silenced, nurtured, embraced, and cuddled. The feeling is like lying with a lover, when time stands still. These are my 'deep' meditations, and while I love when they occur, they are unexpected and very welcome occasions.

When I learned to meditate in high school, I made a deal with my friend Michele. I would go to her house after the classes and teach her everything I learned. I thought it was a very simple technique. They give you a mantra—a sound—and you repeat it to yourself. The problem of passing meditation on to friends is two-fold: 1) the technique is so simple that everyone complicates it; 2) everyone gets a mantra specific to them. I made up a mantra for Michele. So I began meditating daily and enjoying the peace it brought me—and Michele got headaches. After a few months of unsuccessful meditations, Michele took a TM course and began to love meditation.

You can learn meditation from a friend or a book, but you may want to save yourself the headaches and the frustration by taking a class. On your own you might complicate things too much and therefore get frustrated and quit, assuming that you're incapable of meditation. There have been many meditations in which I feel nothing is happening, but in the course of learning TM, I learned not to judge or evaluate my meditations.

Meditation, contrary to popular belief isn't about emptying the mind or always getting to a state of peace. In meditation our thoughts go up and down and fall away at times, just like waves on the ocean. In meditation, we learn to let go of analyzing, thinking, planning, and just be. But thoughts will still find their way in and that is okay. Amazing things happen when we allow ourselves the space to connect to that stillness and not get agitated by our thoughts or judge the process. With meditation we ultimately connect with the depths of our being, with source, with God, with the universe, with consciousness.

In TM they call the field of energy, which connects us all and is within us all, consciousness or the unified field of all the laws of nature. The unified field is what Quantum Physicists speculate is the source of everything, where individuation (and even subatomic particles) ceases and there is pure oneness, pure awareness. When we meditate, we bathe in the divine, in universal energy, and we inevitably bring some of that dynamic peace back with us into our waking state.

In our incredibly busy lives, there is so much to do and to get done. The pace is hectic at times and it can be hard to slow down. I went on a vacation recently. I had gone to the ocean with a "to do" list of sorts. I wanted to read, journal, and think about my life and my direction. But all my mind and body wanted to do was relax and be. We all need a "to be" list. Fortunately, I was lulled back into the moment, into being, just by being by the ocean.

I sometimes think if I just work hard—super hard—I'll be done and suddenly a beautiful clear horizon will stretch out in front of me and I'll be at ease, organic, in my power, and vibrant. But working too hard leads to burnout and even though at some level I want to go non-stop, I stop anyway. I meditate for 20 minutes one to two times a day. I know that with an ongoing meditation practice there is greater light on the horizon, more ease in my being, and greater accomplishments in my life, with less effort and struggle. Meditation may seem unproductive, but it is one of the most productive things we can do on a busy day. One of the meditation gurus says that if you have an especially busy day, then meditate twice as long.

I don't meditate for the pure sake of it; maybe one day I'll return to that. I meditate for the incredible benefits of meditation and because I believe in it philosophically. I am not a model human being; I don't do many of the things I "should" do. But I do know that meditation pays ten-fold so I invest my time in it. With meditation, health improves and aging slows down. Meditation also creates a physiological state that supports happiness, synchronicity, and spiritual attainment. I know that I can expand my consciousness and potential at a faster speed with meditation than I can without it. I want to feel alive and creative and yet relaxed and in a place of trust. Meditation supports me in all of this. I'm not naturally inclined to meditate, but I've made it a practice. I've made a conscious choice to incorporate it into my life.

I remember a conversation with a TM teacher about a year after I first learned to meditate. I was complaining to him about it being hard to schedule meditations and he said, "It's simple Lisa. It is just a decision and you can do it." For five years I didn't miss a meditation. For many reasons for the next few years, I moved away from a regular practice of meditation. Now, at 39, I've made a decision to fit meditation back into my life.

Once you understand what is available to you by regular meditation you won't want to be without it. There are endless benefits to meditation, some subjective, some objective, and some even supernatural. There are over 600 documented scientific studies* showing the many benefits of TM, including how meditation increases creativity, IQ, academic performance, athletic performance, life span, happiness, productivity, self-esteem, longevity, and self-actualization. Transcendental Meditation™ also decreases the incidence of disease, anxiety, insomnia, drug and alcohol use, asthma, high blood pressure, free radicals, arteriosclerosis, depression, reaction time, recidivism and aging, and much more. Researchers can't prove that meditation practitioners are connecting to source, to God, during meditation and they can't prove that meditation brings about more synchronicities. There are some benefits you'll have to test out on your own.

The most intriguing studies have been on the "Maharishi" effect. When we practice meditation, we affect the world around us. We create peace, love, and harmony within our own hearts, and in the quantum fields that connect us all. These waves radiate out, affecting those near and far. There are over 50 documented studies showing that when 1% of a population is practicing TM on an individual basis, or the square root of 1% practices advanced meditation as a group, the quality of life increases. Terrorism, suicide, accidents, illness, and international conflicts decrease substantially. These changes in trend have not been explainable by any other measures. Each of us can make a difference. We can all do something for the world—right from our living room. We can contribute to world peace by bringing ourselves to a space of peace, of stillness.

*These studies have been published in over 100 peer-reviewed scientific and scholarly journals, such as The Journal of Creative Behavior, Social Behavior and Personality, Neuroscience, Journal of Biomedicine, Psychosomatic Medicine, Journal of Counseling and Development, Circulation, and Business and Health.

As an individual, I've meditated on and off for such a long time that it is hard to distinguish what has resulted from meditation or Reiki and what is just part of my nature. I'm generally positive and sometimes idealistic about life. I'm highly intuitive and have experienced clairvoyance at times, as well as precognitive dreams. My life is graced with generosity and with numerous synchronicities. I meet "strangers" that become close friends, or that deliver special messages to me. I feel I have a magical life and my life is blessed with many pleasant surprises and unexpected gifts. I look and feel very young for my age. I'm healthy and medication free, and generally at ease.

I do know that when I'm more centered—a definite outcome of meditation—I feel more connected, both within myself and to others. I'm loving, trusting and open, and less serious. I have less of a desire to control others because when I allow myself to be, I allow others to be. I'm more peaceful. I believe in magic and begin to see evidence of an abundant universe. I feel alive, free, and vibrant again.

Meditation allows us to drink from the fountain of youth. Meditation helps us re-connect with what was natural to us as children—our ability to be in the moment, our natural expressiveness, our spontaneity, our overriding enthusiasm and joy, our sense of limitless possibility. Meditation also literally turns back the clock of time. We get to connect our power cord to the pure supply source and when we do this on a regular basis, cumulative effects happen, like the reversal of aging.

Research on TM has shown that short-term meditators reversed their age by five years, and long-term meditators (meditating twice daily for five years) reversed their age by 12 years. At the age of 40 after five years of meditation, you would have a biological age of 28! This research focused on three markers that deteriorate with time: near-point vision, auditory, and blood pressure. In the composite research of TM, 34 indices have been measured that normally decline with age, but increase in functioning with meditation. I am 39 and I was carded at the liquor store the other day. Yes, I still enjoy a glass of wine or a good cold beer. The man was my age and he looked at my identification and then me and said, "You make me look really old." We turn back the clock of time with meditation.

We also become more efficient with our time. We tap into the fertile ground of all creation and bring that fertility and ease back into our lives and into our actions. Yes, I know we only have so many hours in the day, but when we are more effective, a natural outcome of meditation, we get more done. We do less and accomplish more. But far more exciting than getting more out of our own efforts is having the universe bring needed information, events, and people into our lives at the right moment. Maharishi refers to this grace, these synchronicities, as the "support of nature." These are nature's shortcuts, getting us to our goals faster. Nature is intelligent and whenever possible takes the path of least resistance.

Meditation aligns us with the universe and when we are aligned, our lives flow. We live in sync instead of in friction. We have organization and symmetry surround us instead of chaos. I want to achieve my dreams with the least struggle and effort. I want to apply myself, and infuse my efforts by channeling the creative energy of the universe.

We are meant to continuously learn and grow. We will likely never be "there" or "arrive" because life is about changing and evolving (until we reach enlightenment). The universe will often push us to our next step by offering us a synchronistic event. This event can be a newly opened door or a previously open door that is now closed. Meditation supports us at a fundamental level because it brings us into contact with our being, our higher self, which always knows what we need. When we align with our inner being we naturally bring that alignment into our lives. Of course, we still need to make decisions and take responsibility for our actions. We can't just meditate and then remain passive about our lives. Meditation infuses our actions with more energy and connects us with the organizational power of the universe.

I've had many synchronicities in my life. Some have been so distinct or directive or just plain crazy that I know it was the mind of God at work, bringing people, events, messages, etc. into my life. My work is being taken to the next level because of a synchronicity. I have wanted to produce a guided meditation recording for years, but when I did some research on it, was overwhelmed with the details. The project entails producing the content, the voice recording, the music selection and integration, the artwork, the reproduction, the distribution, and the marketing. In April of 2004, I received an email from a New Age producer who was seeking new artists to work with. He handles every detail of the process. We entered into a joint venture and *Journey Into Meditation: Guided Meditations for Healing, Insight and Manifesting* will be out in 2004.

I am stepping out again. I'm being asked to have a leap of faith and go forward on my new dreams, to take risks. I feel like I'm standing over an abyss with one foot forward and one foot back. The ground on the new frontier isn't firm, it isn't solidified, but my back foot is slipping and the ground is crumbling. It's a strange place to be, but I am willing to embrace the new opportunities being presented to me and meditation reinforces everything I'm doing from a philosophical and a practical perspective.

Even if we meditate everyday, it doesn't take all of our struggles away. I have moments of flow, but lots of moments of fear and resistance, too. I'm not in an ever-present state of bliss. I'm up and down, but I realize there are no limits of time and space and possibility. The universe can figure out some of the details, but we've got to do our part. My part, I believe, is to re-charge my batteries with meditation, to be open to possibilities, and to take action.

Meditation supports us on our life journey and is also a path to higher states of awareness, to enlightenment. But I also know that enlightenment can appear out of nowhere, even by the "smell of the exhaust from a bus." That doesn't mean we should be careless about our lives. We can live consciously and choose a higher road.

What I began to believe after two years of practicing meditation, was that meditation was a path to developing and expanding consciousness and tapping into my potential. According to some experts, it is said that we only use 5-15% of our potential. Why we use such a limited amount of our capacity is a mystery, but we can utilize more of our potential by meditating. In TM, they teach that higher states of consciousness and enlightenment are a natural progression of regular meditation and that consciousness mirrors physiology. They have found in their "yogic flying" program, where advanced practitioners of meditation do a levitation of sorts, a unique state of maximum EEG coherence takes place indicating an orderly and coherent functioning of the brain. Apparently, our physiology is hard-wired to experience and support higher states of consciousness and to go beyond our present capacities.

The effects of meditation build and begin to stick with time. You can't plant a seed and then keep uncovering the dirt to see how it's doing. You water it, fertilize it, give it sun, and know it will grow. This is true with meditation and, for that matter, many good habits or actions taken in the direction of our dreams. You must give them time and undoubtedly you'll experience great benefits. With a solid meditation practice you'll experience benefits beyond your wildest dreams. You'll get younger, and wiser. You'll experience more ease and success in your life and pleasant surprises and synchronicities will be your norm. If you just try it for a few weeks, you'll likely quit. Give your meditation practice a few months to grow and the harvest will be well worth it.

About
Lisa Guyman

As a Life Coach, Reiki Master, and Meditation Teacher, Lisa recognizes the tremendous potential in her fellow human beings that is waiting to be released.

At a young age Lisa became interested in meditation, healing, and personal growth. She followed this interest and graduated with a Bachelors Degree in Psychology emphasizing Philosophy at the University of Michigan. She worked for a wellness company for a short time and then after working for seven years in human resources, she took a leap of faith. She completed massage training, quit her corporate job in Detroit, and moved to Denver in 1997, not knowing anyone there or having a job. Shortly after arriving she rented an office space and started her massage and energy healing practice, Inner Sanctum.

Several months later she began offering and then teaching Reiki, a Japanese form of energy healing. Through Reiki she has witnessed many profound transformations in her students and clients. She has taught Reiki to over 400 people and continues to offer Reiki workshops.

Lisa's passion lies in teaching, and also in supporting people in the pursuit of their dreams and goals. In 2001, she crossed paths with several life coaches and realized that coaching would allow her to work on this authentic and purposeful level with people. Lisa completed the Coaching from Spirit program in early 2002 and began her work as a coach. She offers both in-person and tele-coaching.

Growth often requires taking new risks. Lisa is in the process of quantum growth in her life and thus has started new ventures. She is embracing opportunities and sacrificing security to follow her dreams.

Lisa's vision is to positively affect as many lives as possible and contribute to world peace. She believes her purpose is to bring more light and love into the world and to support people in realizing their potential and re-awakening to all that they are. Her mission is to support people in expanding and deepening their connection to source while empowering them to unfold their dreams and live a fulfilling, purposeful life.

She seeks to accomplish her mission by providing sanctuary for people and by communicating spiritual and practical tools and concepts through her workshops, one-on-one sessions, speaking engagements, writing, and guided meditations.

Since meditation has been core to her life and since she believes meditation is one of the most beneficial things anyone can do for their lives and for the world, she was thrilled with the opportunity to write about the benefits of meditation and to publish her first writing in *A Guide to Getting It: Sacred Healing*. Lisa's CD recording, *Journey into Meditation: Guided Meditations for Healing, Insight and Manifesting* will be released in late 2004.

To contact Lisa, call 303-725-1023 or email lisaguyman@prodigy.net. To view her products, class offerings, or to book her for a speaking engagement or workshop, visit www.inner-sanctum.com.

Leading With Your Heart

By Kathleen Thompson

Ram Das says, "Healing is what brings us closer to God. Healing moves us closer to the One, and if you're the One then you're whole . . . that's the ultimate in healing . . . making whole." Until a few years ago my definition of healing was about something being wrong with someone and getting fixed, better, cured, etc. Certainly not something I ever thought I needed; always somebody else, but never me. But my experiences the last few years have changed my perspective about many things, including my understanding of healing. As I prepared to write this chapter, it occurred to me that my journey has actually been one I consider a Sacred Healing—coming to wholeness from the inside out.

That journey began in October 1999. I was on a plane on my way home from the United Kingdom. Big changes were coming with my company being acquired by a British firm, the second buyout in the short time frame of only a year. I had traveled frequently the few years prior to this moment, but putting aside the hassle of it all, I truly loved the solitude of air travel. It was my escape, because no one could reach me while I was in the air. When I was in the plane, I had the time to just be with me without responsibility for anyone else. But tonight would be somewhat different and would change the direction of my life dramatically.

I had put my heart and soul into this corporation for 29 years. However, for the three years leading to this night, something had changed. At times I felt numb, restless, uncaring, and even irresponsible. But how could this have happened? After all, I was the top Human Resources executive of this now global entity! As a single parent of two children for 17 years, I had climbed the so-called corporate ladder, something that seemed to happen without my actually planning it that way. I was independent, self-sufficient, and seemingly successful, so what was the problem?

Well, for one thing I had always suffered from a lack of self-confidence, never truly believing in myself. Yet as each new challenge entered my life, I somehow managed to deal with it. But the crossroad I now found myself at was different. Where before I was always concerned and worried about how I would be perceived and if I could really do what had to be done, this time I found myself just not caring—at all. For the first time in my professional life, my corporate responsibilities just didn't seem important when I thought of them as an aspect of my life. To tell the truth, at that point it didn't even feel like I had a life—because it was all wrapped up in the corporation. I was the proverbial hamster on the wheel, and I had begun to feel so physically exhausted that even my usual energy for my regular exercise routine had failed me.

Although I now know that my body was giving me warning signals, at the time I was so out of touch with that part of me, that I didn't have a clue to the messages it was sending me. I felt a strong sense of wanting to make more of a difference with people than I felt I was making, and I no longer had any tolerance for the daily bureaucracy in which I lived. Being in the executive ranks had taken me away from interacting with regular employees, being a trouble-shooter, helping, and being of service. Emotionally, I often felt desperately alone and not connected with others, whether family, female friends, or business associates. But I was incapable of showing any vulnerability. Being needy was not the image I ever wanted to project. I always felt I had to appear competent, in control, and able to handle anything that came my way—the Superwoman syndrome, big-time. I also felt disconnected from the real me—the business-suit-and-heels person versus the one in workout clothes. Those images of myself were actually two entirely different people. So how could I connect with the latter and make a more meaningful life for myself?

For some time, I had been wrestling with the possibility of leaving the corporation. But when strong emotions came up, instead of facing them, I became adept at avoiding them. However, something inside me kept bringing the subject up until finally I knew the time had come to make a decision. My time on the plane trip was the answer, I thought. I would make a simple list of pros and cons about leaving. I would be objective and realistic and view all aspects of my life as I made my list. So I did just that, and within a very short time I found my Pro list quite a bit longer than my Con list. Gosh it felt good to see that! Did I already know in my heart that's what I wanted to do? The answer is yes, but at the time all I knew was that something deep within me released and I felt totally at peace—no fear, no lack of confidence, just a sweet peace.

As an adult I had no religious practice in my life and the closest I came to spirituality was my once-a-week yoga class with a short meditation at the end. But that night my decision just felt so right, with absolutely no fear of what lay ahead for me, that I now believe it was some kind of spiritual intervention or awakening.

Three months later, in January 2000, during a major snowstorm, I left my job. My body was exhausted. I felt fat and lethargic. I also felt an incredible feeling of liberation in leaving my job of 29 years. It was amazing to me how ready I was to let go of it. I didn't miss anything about the place or my work. I'd never felt so free in my entire life. I had the world before me and I could literally create my life now. I read some inspiring books and just hunkered down in the middle of winter. I found that my elderly father and aging dog needed much more of my attention (and compassion), and now I had the time for them without the demands and stress of my corporate job. I was also fortunate to have a financial cushion that would allow me to take a year or so to figure out what I would do with the rest of my life.

My salvation during my corporate years was exercise. It relieved my stress, gave me energy, and kept me fit and healthy. It also somewhat satisfied my driving need to always look good. I worked in a defense company, for the most part a man's world, and so I thought being attractive was just as important as being dependable. I put a lot of pressure on myself about my appearance or "external self" and how I thought people perceived me or expected me to look, and be, in the positions I held. My focus was always about how I was *supposed* to be versus how I really was (on the inside). And it was always about never being quite good enough.

In 1996, having read about the growing popularity of yoga, I decided to try it to improve my flexibility. I started to attend a weekly class. I loved it from the start and never missed a session. Yoga made me more aware of my body. I enjoyed the lengthening, the opening, as well as the peace of mind. The session always ended with a 15-minute meditation, which I silently reasoned wasn't necessary for me. Eventually I tried it and found it made a huge difference. I felt more in touch with my inner self. I was kinder to people and I found myself smiling more. When we meditated, it felt like time stopped. I felt a link to something bigger than myself. That type of nurturing made me feel good inside—and good about my world.

After leaving my job, I felt a strong desire to delve further into yoga. My yoga class had become so precious to me. It revived me physically, mentally, and yes, spiritually. Was it a lack of spirituality that I was feeling/ lacking/longing for? And what was spirituality anyway? I wanted a connection with God, but it wasn't anything related to religion or my Catholic upbringing. What I think my heart was longing for was a deeper connection with myself, touching the true nature that had eluded me much of my life. In the silence, concentration, and focus of yoga practice and all that it encompassed, I felt a closer alignment with my true self—and the divinity within my own being. I could honor my goodness and worthiness knowing I had something of value to offer to others.

I also wanted a deeper connection with people. I decided to take a short teacher training, not thinking I could possibly be a yoga teacher, but that it would give me more of the philosophical foundation of the practice. Although I had no plan to become a teacher, something drew me there. My gremlins appeared, whispering to me that I compare myself to the others in the class who were already teaching. But, in finishing the course, I learned more of the philosophy and left wanting more. It resonated with me. The need to live from the inside out was beginning to unfold—and I had no clue!

Shortly after I finished the class, being an outdoor biking enthusiast, I decided to do a group biking tour in Italy, where I had maternal roots. And off I went—by myself— for the adventure of my life—and it truly was. I soon found myself doing yoga at 6 A.M. in the hill towns of central Italy. Practicing yoga during the trip was magical; it definitely connected my body and mind. I didn't know it then but that trip was living my values: nature, health, connection with people, and yoga/spirituality. I wrote in my journal and did yoga almost every day. I was moving my body and opening my heart to all I loved. It was heavenly.

With the bike trip and teacher training under my belt, I began to feel the need to get back to the reality of a moneymaking job. Upon my return from Italy I read about something called Life Coaching. It seemed to have some spiritual underpinnings, and it reminded me of yoga philosophy. I talked to an old friend who had become a coach and she referred me to the training program she had gone through. The ever practical, logical me was skeptical, with a lot of doubt about the direction I was taking. But I listened to my heart, and trusting my intuition, signed up for the training. I paid close to $4,000 and off I went to California. The training was my first experience with a "spiritually oriented" program. I left with more self-love, acceptance of people, and excitement about sharing all this with others as a Life Coach. I also practiced yoga every day, which contributed to my overall experience. When I looked at what coaching was, I was reminded of the same things yoga provided: a connection and oneness with others and a love and acceptance of self, and the Divine within that self.

The coach training brought a major shift in my life—a conscious connection with the Divine that heretofore had been unconscious for most of my life. I suddenly started seeing people differently and valuing things in a new way. Emotionally, I let the vulnerable me come through in front of people I hardly knew. I started to learn more about my values, and how those values showed up in my life. Prior to that time I had never thought about what I truly valued, much less about how much those values were realized in the various aspects of my life. The process has taught me much about self-awareness, which of course is what coaching is all about. So I became a coach! I started to market myself to find clients—not so easy for one who had been held in the arms of a large corporation for most of her life.

Meanwhile, I discovered a new yoga studio and decided to try it—and loved it! The style, Anusara Yoga, was new to me, but synchronicity was at play here. I had named my business Follow Your Heart Coaching, and this new style of yoga I found (or had it found me?) translated to "following your heart." I knew this was where I was supposed to be! I had always had an affinity for hearts and the symbolism of heart being the core was strong. I never used to think of things like this before the coach training and my further exploration into yoga. Thinking of a spiritual guidance or even divine intervention was just not me (or so I thought).

I continued coaching my half dozen clients and practicing yoga, but something was still missing. The end of the year was approaching, so I decided to go on my own to a five-day silent yoga retreat. I spent the week between Christmas and New Year's away from celebrations, friends, and family, going deeper to find myself. I was still being pulled inside to find the answers my heart was seeking.

A few months after starting at the yoga studio, I discovered they offered a teacher-training program and, much to my surprise, I signed up for it. I was really going to become a yoga teacher! Unfortunately, my fears of failure and public speaking reared their ugly heads and I struggled with staying in my heart and not my head. But thanks to my coach training, what I lacked in knowing and technique somehow gave way to a belief in myself, and the confidence that I could teach yoga despite my fears. So I subbed in some classes. I paid attention to my body and its feelings. I noticed when I felt best after a class and when I didn't. When I felt good was when I let go of my thoughts of the students' perception of me—how I looked and sounded. When I didn't feel so good, it was all about what I was getting or not getting, instead of what I was giving to them. Letting the light of my heart shine out to them energetically and speaking and acting from my heart—that's when I felt my teaching was at its finest. More opportunities to teach came and with it more confidence, which now felt more like an inner glow. I began to love preparing for the class, executing it, and finding that balanced place of comfort in the flow and timing of each class. I also loved interacting with the students and delighted in their compliments about my teaching. It was all sort of like dance choreography. A life dance perhaps, but what I found is that it was teaching from my heart, my core, my true nature, and it just felt so right.

As teaching increased, coaching lagged, and I lost any semblance of confidence I had in my coaching because of long periods with no clients. I spent more money taking different types of coach training here and there, but none of it seemed to make a difference in my getting clients. I enrolled in another coaching school where I found great training, teachers, and more wonderful people wanting to become coaches. In fact, the coaching community was as wonderful as the yoga teacher community. But yoga was still the big passion in my life.

As I continued my study of yoga, I was drawn to articles in Yoga Journal written by a man who was a part of the Insight Meditation community. He wrote of yoga and the heart that I felt in a deep way. I decided to find a local Insight Meditation group and in January 2003, I attended a session—by myself once again. Hmm, seems when I follow my heart into something new or different, I go it alone—and it usually leads to more meaning in my life.

Well, there I am sitting cross-legged on the floor of a lovely Unitarian Church with maybe 200-300 people in the room with me. We started the meditation and the room became silent, slowly, until you could hear a pin drop. I was in silence with all these people, but the silence was speaking volumes. The realization that we were all there for the same purpose—going within ourselves to somehow live a more meaningful life—totally overwhelmed me and filled me with such a sense of coming home. I was choked with emotion. The dharma talk was equally inspiring, as was the teacher who spoke. I floated home on a cloud of "ahhhhhh." I knew I would keep going back and that this type of meditation was the method for me right now.

I continued to teach and study yoga, meditate, do more teacher trainings, and a little bit of coaching. I was frustrated with my coaching and lack of clients, but nothing I did seemed to change that. The fear of failing as a coach kept rearing its head, but instead of listening to that gremlin, I chose to believe and trust that something would eventually change and that coaching had come into my life for a reason. This wasn't about my not being a good coach; rather it was about a different way coaching would manifest itself in my life. I truly felt the coaching and yoga would come together in some way and that would be my path for the future.

Early in 2003 my yoga studio announced it was being sold. The words hit me like a bolt of lightning going directly through my body. I literally felt a fire within me. I knew at that moment I wanted to buy it—I wanted to combine my business knowledge with my love of teaching yoga and share this wonderful spiritual practice with more and more people. I could even introduce people to coaching through the studio! There was such a confidence in my heart that I could do this. If there was one thing I had learned the past two years it was practicing what I preached about listening to the voice of the heart, and additionally the "voice" of the body. I had actually heard this message previously (from within myself) about opening my own yoga studio, but I had dismissed it thinking I wasn't a good enough teacher. Well this time was different and I realized how much I wanted this, and how aligned it was with all my values. So I began the process to make a bid. In the end, the studio owner changed her mind and decided not to sell.

By that time there was no deterring me from this road so, with the help of a commercial broker, I began looking for space. This took longer than I thought it would. Through many months I was often frustrated and discouraged, but I felt strongly—an inner knowing—that this was what I was supposed to do. I knew I had to trust my heart and just let things happen in their own time. And then the day came when I found my space! It was love at first sight. I mulled it over for a few days, but I knew from the minute I saw it that this was the space. Three months later, appropriately on Valentine's Day, I opened my Yoga Center doors, and with that opening a new chapter of my life began. Every day now I wake up happy and excited to have a new day in which to share with others what the Center offers, which essentially is bringing people home to their hearts.

Coming to Wholeness: Physical, Mental, Emotional, and Spiritual Healing

So what makes my story one of *Sacred Healing*? If healing is coming to wholeness and wholeness is containing all the parts, then I believe my healing touched all of me, the physical, mental, emotional, and spiritual—and all as a result of meditation, yoga, coach training, and coaching. My healing has been like a slow, revered shift to a feeling of wholeness; the deep longing being satiated at last, maybe not fully, but coming closer every day—it's a life journey really.

My physical healing was about gaining a greater respect for my physical body and its connection with the subtle and divine energies within it, and the reality that my body speaks to me through its signals of discomfort and pain. "Listening to" and often "being with" the sensations and feelings of my body is vital to my well being. In the past year I have also experienced acupuncture and truly believe in its healing ability to unblock the subtle energy channels within the body to bring it back into balance. I have learned too that my own yoga practice can be an offering or form of devotion using my body to express myself through the physical movement of the yoga poses. In Anusara Yoga we call this "opening to grace"—allowing one's divinity to shine out to celebrate life through the body.

Mentally the healing has come in the form of greater clarity and awareness, and that awareness is even keener when I am living in the present moment versus the past or the future. I have discovered that overwhelm and stress (and even forgetfulness!) come from not living in the moment, but rather worrying about something in the yesterdays or tomorrows. That doesn't mean one can't plan and be responsible, but all we really know is this moment, so detaching from a future that may not come is a far healthier and freer way to live a fulfilling life.

Emotionally the healing has been in peeling back the layers to uncover what is stopping me from being confident and moving ahead. These "obstacles" may manifest in the form of disappointment, self-doubt, anger, judgment, and frustration, but the bottom layer is pure and simple fear. If I can be with that emotion, feel it in my body and know it, and still love myself, then I can move past it and forward. The embodiment of the feeling is the road to healing.

Spiritually, this healing has been huge. I know this piece of me wasn't missing, but perhaps just dormant. My consciousness of it now has been awakened to the point that I would really feel incomplete today if I couldn't tap into this source of peace and harmony within me. Although meditation is my greatest resource to connect spiritually, I do try to live my life every day leading with my heart, my spiritual core. I now have a far stronger feeling of connection with others, a deep respect for the divinity of others, and the knowing we are not so different or separate from one another. Basically we are striving for the same thing—to be happy.

The Foundation of Anusara Yoga: Attitude, Alignment, and Action

As I write about my own *Sacred Healing*, I realize that I am now truly living the foundation principles I practice and teach in Anusara Yoga. Those foundation pieces are: **Attitude, Alignment,** and **Action**—and all three are interconnected.

Attitude is first and the most important. In Anusara Yoga we often refer to it as the power of the heart that is the force behind the action and energetic feel of each pose. From a spiritual perspective it is our aspiration to re-awaken to our divine nature and thus celebrate life. Bhava is Sanskrit for feeling, attitude, or conviction. When you consciously set the intention—your bhava—this is the source of your own energetic expression of the poses. Taking this same feeling or intention "off the mat" can bring that same energy to whatever you want to do in your life—it brings with it the confidence and empowerment to be your true self, and to celebrate that!

Alignment is the mindful knowing of how the various parts of ourselves are integrated and interconnected. In yoga, when we align our bodies to our own "optimal blueprint," the poses feel good, and with our bodies more open and free we are often able to go beyond where our mind says we can. And that's empowering! In life, alignment comes from being grounded in what we believe—our values—those innate qualities we hold deep in our hearts that define our true nature. And when those values are being totally honored and realized, we have a sense of peace and an all-is-right-with-the-world feeling. This then gives us the courage to step into the power of our heart to realize our true desires.

Finally, there is **Action**. In Anusara Yoga, when the Attitude and Alignment are realized, then the Action is one of balanced energetic movement in which the whole body, mind, and spirit participate. It's the icing on the cake—the physical manifestation of willpower. It is a stepping into the natural flow and pulse of life and an opening to joyful freedom.

Self-Love and Freedom

There is another word in Sanskrit that I love—it is maitri. Maitri translates to loving kindness or unconditional friendliness and relates to our relationship with our self. Maitri is a self-honoring; so rather than pushing ourselves to be better, greater—different than we are—it's making friends with who we really are. Doing this is letting go of that constant struggle to be different than we are, and accepting and loving ourselves. Self-honoring is about being good enough—because we already are and always have been.

My cultivation of this attitude of maitri has given me so much—the gift of realizing my gifts: My teaching, my coaching, my writing, my yoga practice—and so much more. I like to think that my path to self-love brought me to a truly divine moment, a few months ago now, when for the umpteenth time in over two years I attempted to do a handstand at the wall. Only this particular time up I went! There I was, upside-down and standing on my hands, and it was the most glorious feeling of freedom and empowerment I have ever felt. Accomplishing that movement represented for me much more than a physical feat—I was at a crossroad again, but this time I knew how I got there, where I was, and most important, where I was going...

About
Kathleen Thompson

Kathleen Thompson, R.Y.T., began coaching after completing a 29-year corporate career in Human Resources Management. She left that career having absolutely no idea what she would do next. Then something she had never heard of before appeared—something called Coaching. She was immediately drawn to it, explored it, talked to others about it, and eventually decided to take the training, without knowing exactly how she would apply it. But she was intrigued by the thought of having her own business and being her own boss. At the end of her first coach-training program the name of her business came to her—Follow Your Heart Coaching. And that has been her journey since then: Answering the call of her heart with conscious awareness. In her coaching business, Kathleen works mainly with women, guiding them to align their lives with their deepest values and inner wisdom.

Upon approaching the age of 50, Kathleen took up the practice of yoga, taking a weekly two-hour class. Initially she intended to become more flexible, but as time went by something shifted. Each class ended with 15 minutes of meditation that, combined with the movement of the body through the poses, brought a sweet inner peace. Leaving the corporate world, Kathleen found she longed to learn more about yoga. She soon discovered a style of Hatha yoga called Anusara Yoga. She loved the combination of the biomechanical body alignment principles and the heart-oriented language. She soon found, to her astonishment, that Anusara is a Sanskrit word meaning "follow your heart." Soon thereafter a teacher training became available and again, the call from her heart was to take it. Six months later she was teaching yoga.

From her early experience with meditation, Kathleen continued to explore different types. She was ultimately drawn to the Buddhist practice known as Vipassana or Mindfulness Meditation. Although not schooled in Buddhist philosophy and principles, Mindfulness Meditation resonated with her heart-oriented way of life, as well as with her coaching and yoga teaching.

Kathleen opened her own Anusara yoga center in early 2004 and plans to introduce both coaching and mindfulness meditation to her students as she guides them to live from the wisdom of their hearts.

To contact Kathleen, email coach@fyhcoaching.com, call 301-972-4784, or visit www.followyourheartyoga.com or www.followyourheartcoaching.com.

Laugh Two Times and Call Me in the Morning: Using Humor for Balance and Healing

By Rick Garrison

"THE HUMAN RACE HAS ONLY ONE REALLY EFFECTIVE WEAPON, AND THAT'S LAUGHTER. THE MOMENT IT ARISES, ALL OUR HARDNESSES YIELD, ALL OUR IRRITATIONS AND RESENTMENTS SLIP AWAY, AND A SUNNY SPIRIT TAKES THEIR PLACE." ~ MARK TWAIN

Laughter as Medicine, Creating Balance for Healing

Humor and laughter are wonderful drugs. In my sixteen years of nursing experience I know of no one who has ever overdosed on either. I have experienced bad humor, where making jokes goes beyond satire and becomes cynicism, but good humor, laughing, chuckling, and even smiling, enhances and encourages healing. Joy, wonder, and lightness are at the heart of this powerful medicine, an antidote to fear, sadness, and anything else that causes stress. Humor and laughter lead to joy, and that is where healing miracles begin.

As children we see the world with fresh eyes; we hold it all in wonder. Every experience tickles our fancy. When we are infants, even though we do not like it when our pants need changing or we are hungry or tired, we are generally pretty happy because everything is new. We are able to be in a constant state of awe. This state of wonder is a gift from the divine. However, as adults, we often lose sight of how much fun there is in life, and struggle to get that feeling of lightness back.

Humor and laughter are also divine gifts. In the book of Proverbs Chapter 17, Verse 22, we are told, "A cheerful heart is a good medicine, but a downcast spirit dries up the bones." Like the other authors in this book, I believe healing is sacred. Embracing that understanding is necessary if we are to truly restore ourselves to complete health. In the simplest way, those gifts of wonder, humor, and laughter open us to the divine energy of the universe, attracting powers beyond what we see to help us operate with ease in our lives, and to promote that Sacred Healing.

A sense of humor is one of our greatest assets. It is the ability to see things in a certain light and in a funny way. It can create new perspectives and can be applied to any subject or situation. My personal belief is that the divine energy of the universe (what I also refer to as "spirit" or the life force that is in all things) has the greatest sense of humor. I use mosquitoes as proof. Others might say God has a sense of humor because She created men. How could you not love a God that likes a good joke? Charles Shultz, the creator of the cartoon *Peanuts*, said, "Nobody would have been invited to dinner as much as Jesus was unless he was interesting and had a sense of humor."

The use of humor is so valuable that most cultures have clowns and comedians, those most important members who reflect fun and humor back to us. Civilizations also have mythical stories or legends of tricksters, characters that show us how to laugh at ourselves. Humans have recognized for ages that the healing of communities is as important as the healing of individuals. Our humor "guides," those clowns and tricksters, jesters and comedians provide the medicine.

Having a sense of humor becomes vitally important when we experience illness or injury, our own, or if we have to bear witness to someone else's distress. There are always unwanted circumstances that can happen to us, some life changing or life threatening. In addition to the physical stress that we often have to manage, there is also mental, emotional, and spiritual strain. In many cases, the non-physical is the worst. A sense of humor and the desire to experience joy in life are great defenses in the face of sadness, grief, and fear. Laughter gives us more room to accept what comes our way.

Humor and laughter cannot make pain or suffering go away, but they can make it manageable and more bearable. Having these in our life is the counter-weight that brings us back into balance. When balance happens, all the power the universe has to offer can be accessed, wholeness can be achieved, and healing happens.

Humor is the recognition and expression of incongruities or peculiarities present in a situation or character. Laughter is a physical response to that humorous situation. Humor is the thought and laughter is a tangible result of that view. Humor is looking for fun. Laughter is finding it. Humor and laughter have a "chicken or egg" relation to each other. What is first doesn't really matter. Laughter connects us to our sense of humor, and humor leads us to laughter. Laughter also leads us to joy, and joy opens us up to love. To be open to love is to be open to the sacred. Being open to the sacred is allowing the divine to be present in our lives. The divine is what makes miracles possible. This then, is the powerful energy medicine of laughter and humor.

Laughing Himself to Life: Balancing Humor and Laughter with Modern Medicine in Self-Healing

"A HUMAN BEING IS NOT A MACHINE AND ONLY A HUMAN BEING HAS A BUILT-IN MECHANISM FOR REPAIRING ITSELF, FOR MINISTERING TO ITS OWN NEEDS, AND FOR COMPREHENDING WHAT IS HAPPENING TO IT. THE REGENERATIVE AND RESTORATIVE FORCE IN HUMAN BEINGS IS AT THE CORE OF HUMAN UNIQUENESS." ~ NORMAN COUSINS, FROM 'ANATOMY OF AN ILLNESS, AS PERCEIVED BY THE PATIENT'

One of the best-known stories about healing with the science of laughter, humor, and joy, is that of Norman Cousins. Norman Cousins is famous for having overcome a bleak diagnosis with the use of laughter. It is said he laughed himself from death's doorstep back to health, life, and vitality. His story shows how humor and laughter can bring balance to your life and promote healing.

Although the best known fact of this story is Cousins' use of laughter as part of his treatment plan, laughing and feeling good were not all that returned him to health. He believed the full range of positive emotions were an important part of an overall treatment plan, alongside modern medical treatment and drugs.

Cousins' response to his illness was to be an active participant in his own healing. He read as much as he could about how his disease affected him. What he discovered was a significant amount of research on how the negative emotions of fear, grief, and sadness had a harmful effect on a person's health and ability to heal, but nothing on the positive emotions' impact on health or healing. He reasoned that if negative emotions had a negative effect on a person's health, then the opposite must be true. He had his friend, Allan Funt, the producer and creator of *Candid Camera*, send him film reels of the show, along with a movie projector. After viewing those episodes, he followed them with Marx Brothers' movies, funny books, and stories—anything that would make him laugh. The illness caused him pain in all his joints. Even sleeping was painful. Yet, he found that after ten minutes of genuine belly laughter he was able to get two hours of pain-free sleep. This amazing fact, even though it is only anecdotal, caused the modern medical community to take note. The only negative effect of this treatment was that he was disturbing other patients!

At the onset of his symptoms, a sedimentation rate, a blood test that indicates inflammation or infection, was collected from him. This test was repeated periodically. As his symptoms became worse, the sedimentation rate increased. By the time he was admitted to a hospital, it had skyrocketed through the roof. When he started the laughter therapy, he also started taking larger than normal doses of Vitamin C. As his symptoms decreased and he was able to get increasingly longer periods of sleep, his sedimentation rate dropped. This showed a physical response to the treatment. Laughter was a large part of his self-directed plan. Along with the use of Vitamin C, he was able to overcome the disease and return to health.

Norman Cousins also wrote the forward to the book, *Live Longer through Laughter*, by Joey Adams. In that forward, he wrote, "Some of the comments about a book I wrote under the title *Anatomy of an Illness* made it appear that I laughed my way out of a serious health condition. Careful readers of the book, however, knew my emphasis was on the full range of positive emotions and their vital importance in an effective partnership between patient and physician. Laughter—along with hope, faith, love, the will to live, creativity—can be regarded as an important resource in any strategy of recovery or, indeed, in prompting good health."

Mr. Cousins' story raised public awareness of the effect of emotional factors on health and healing, especially the positive effect of laughter. This story also speaks to the relationship a patient has with doctors, hospitals, and the modern medical community or system.

Using Humor and Laughter to Help Others Heal

In Cousins' statement he says, "My emphasis was on the full range of positive emotions and their vital importance in an *effective partnership between patient and physician*."

The relationship between patient and physician has been found to be the most important part of healing. This relationship requires there to be a solid trust between the two parties for optimal healing to occur. The patient/healer relationship has been sacred in all cultures—until now. When the patient/healer relationship is poor, the patient is dissatisfied and the caregiver experiences frustration. Building trust is easier when people can laugh together, making humor and laughter a valuable tool in building this or any other relationship.

One of the biggest reasons more people are going to alternative therapy providers is for the relationship that is part of this type of treatment. Alternative providers spend more time with their patients and create a connection quickly. There is a relaxed atmosphere that reduces tension and builds trust. Alternative therapy providers also understand the use of energy in healing and understand the powerful effect it has on well-being and health.

Too often in mainstream medicine, the patient/doctor relationship has become a brief interaction. Often, neither patient nor physician knows each other very well. The use of humor can play an integral role in developing and supporting a strong relationship. Steven M. Sultanoff, Ph.D. states, "We feel good when we experience humor. Humor can act as a 'social lubricant' by decreasing interpersonal tension and offering perspective on life's stressors. For the relationship between patient and physician to be able to fully facilitate healing, both must feel good in it."

Developing a relationship with your doctor is not like trying to become best friends. The dynamic must be professional—and, you need to "feel good in it." This creates an atmosphere of trust so that when difficult, sad events or health concerns come up, they can be talked about openly.

I use humor for building relationships—and it works. As a nurse, I have more time to be with patients than physicians generally do. The patient is in a vulnerable circumstance. Trust needs to be established between the patient and myself quickly for optimum delivery of care. When I meet a patient and the timing is such that I think I will get at least a chuckle, my first line is, "If you laugh at my jokes, you have been here too long and it's time for you to go home." I watch the patient's reaction and begin assessing their sense of humor. I use humor to lighten up the moment—forging the beginning of the relationship—and make the point that I want him or her to get well and go home as soon as possible. This demonstrates to the patient that I am on the same side and it changes the vibration or feeling of the moment. It helps me assess if my patient wants to—or can—laugh at the situation they are in.

My other line is, "We are not known for our cuisine, entertainment, or fashion sense." The timing for that line usually coincides with meal times. Hospital food does have a reputation, so why not make a joke of it? The other time that is good for that line is when I am helping a patient put on one of those famous hospital gowns.

I've learned to trust my instincts about how and when to use my sense of humor, not just as a nurse interacting with a patient, but with all people. I become aware of what the other person's sense of humor is in that moment. Meeting people wherever they are is important. Using humor equalizes the status between people, thereby empowering both. It bridges barriers and even polarities that occur between people.

Recently on an afternoon shift, I took care of a patient another nurse was responsible for in the morning, but when he came back from a morning procedure, he was assigned to my care. I noticed he was not in a very good mood. He was crabby, complaining about everything, including our schedule, the fact that he couldn't have food, and so on. As I was attaching the monitoring equipment to him, he asked questions about what was going on and if he was going to be able to eat.

I replied, "This is how I get patients to like me. I wait until they've been starved, then I eventually become their nurse and bring them food and they think I'm a hero." He chuckled a little and asked again about food. I told him, "The downside of being the person to bring you food is that it's hospital food and when you get it I may not be such a hero." Then I had to explain to him that he will be stuck in bed for another nine hours and that in a couple of hours the catheter in the artery of his leg will come out and I will be putting two hundred pounds (my weight) on that spot to make sure the bleeding stops. He was thrilled to hear that.

Using humor is a part of developing trust and helps diffuse the seriousness of the situation. Humor in this case shifted the patient's attention to outside of himself. My use of humor gave the message that "this is a passing situation and we are going to help you get through it."

Working with humor as a nurse, I constantly attune to the needs of the patient. My experience is that keeping things light when possible helps make a patient's stay shorter and not quite as scary. Of course I have to be careful how I use humor because of the vulnerability of the patient and the patient's family. Being in the hospital is frightening and it is often even more so for family members.

Individuals get through health crises faster and easier if humor is a part of their coping mechanism. Keeping things light, telling jokes, being on the lookout for what brings humor and fun into any situation are important skills. We all have the ability to be clowns; it starts with the ability to see the absurd in a situation and then magnify it for others. Red rubber nose is optional.

The Healing Role of Clowns and Tricksters

"A PHYSICIANS ROLE IS TO ENTERTAIN AND HUMOR THE PATIENT WHILE NATURE HEALS THEM." ~ VOLTAIRE

We have all been exposed to the archetype of the trickster. In school they were the "Class Clowns." In our adult life they are the stand-up comics and comedic actors, or even talk show hosts. They bring humor into our lives, often at the expense or chagrin of authority. Whether it is a class clown, office clown, or professional comic, those that are successful and well known are the ones who know the rules and maintain the fine line that society has drawn regarding what is acceptable. Clowns are like a mirror that reflects our image back to us, showing us how we take ourselves too seriously.

Laughter and humor are a part of all cultures. Through the figures of clowns and tricksters and their stories, people have been finding things to laugh at throughout history. Clowns, tricksters, and contraries have the role of bringing balance to the entire community they serve. This balance comes from their ability to bring laughter and the perspective of the absurd so the people can see it, especially during difficult times. Being able to see the absurd in life is wise and fosters healing. Those who have the ability to help others see the incongruities of life are often honored as wise people, the ones who can guide a community through difficult times.

Tricksters and clowns are both symbolic and actual bearers of mirth and absurdity. They represent the balanced perspective we need to have with the full spectrum of emotions: joy, sadness, happiness, and fear. Tricksters and clowns represent the balance of the reverent and the irreverent. Clowns, as bearers of fun and humor, are best known for their performance and antics at circuses. The tricksters we find in mythology are born of divine creative power and demonstrate the absurd nature of creation.

Jesters, clowns, or fools were part of most royal courts. They had the ability to say things to kings the rest of the court could not. They had the job of making people laugh, especially at parties and banquets. Although jesters and minstrels performed primarily for royalty and nobility, folklore tells of them going into the community and bringing fun and joy to all. Their influence and impact was on community well-being and healing and not on the healing of individuals (except for the king). The common people had to entertain themselves. Considering the stories that have survived with the horrible images of the way things were in the distant past, there wasn't much to laugh about.

The emperor of China who built the Great Wall had the idea to paint it so it would look better. The members of his court were afraid to say anything to him because to contradict him could be fatal. The court jester, a clown named Yu Sze, made fun of the emperor, showing the absurdity of his idea. Thousands of lives were lost building the Great Wall. Thousands more could have been lost painting it. It took a clown to save a thousand lives.

The best known trickster in many North American legends is Coyote. In the book and card deck *Medicine Cards*, by Jamie Sams and David Carson, they write, "If coyote is coming your way you can be sure some kind of medicine is on its way . . . Coyote always comes calling when you are taking yourself too seriously. The medicine is in laughter and joking so that new view points may be assumed." Coyote definitely shows up in my life at those times when I am taking things and myself too seriously. If I forget and get too serious again, he knows where I live.

Laughter and Humor as Alternative Medicine

My research and experience tell me most modern medical providers still discount alternative medicine, what I like to call "energy medicine" such as Qigong, Reiki, and healing touch. Modern medicine is based on fixing the machine we call the body. Energy medicine therapies are based on the scientific fact that all things are energy. Everything in our universe vibrates at various levels.

Joy and humor are "light" and "high" vibrations. As mentioned earlier, these vibrations are closely related to the divine. Humor changes the vibration of tense situations, opening up the heart to joy. Bringing joy into daily life is an essential part of feeling happy, having a sense of well being, and experiencing a deep connection to the sacred. Joy requires us to find what tickles our funny bone, what makes us smile, what causes us to fall to the ground doubled over in laughter. Joy can be brought into life with smiles, flowers, cards, recognition—anything happy, even in sad situations. Joy and happiness are fluid emotions and help us move through experiences of fear, sadness, and pain of any type.

On the other hand, sadness and fear hold us back. When we feel stuck and unable to move, when we feel unable to create the lives we want, we are usually succumbing to fear or sadness. It weighs us down. Many of life's challenges are expressed as a journey from darkness to light. Joy and happiness are the light we are all reaching for. When darkness comes, we can move through it and overcome it by using humor to create joy. Joy is the window to the love the universe has for us. When we are wrapped in the love of the universe we connect to everything, we are whole; it is where we find healing and peace. The journey of healing is a journey to wholeness. It is an individual path, and yet we are not alone. With humor we fortify ourselves and enlist allies, both physical and spirit.

Humor and laughter is energy healing that can be used by everyone. No training is required!

Practice Makes Perfect—Start Now

Humor and laughter are powerful medicine. Like muscles, you need to use them to keep them strong and healthy. Regular humor and laughter exercise is the best way to prepare for a time you might really need or want to access it for its healing properties. Start here:

- Know your own sense of humor and what makes you laugh. Explore what tickles your funny bone, what makes you smile. Think about the most hilarious thing you have ever experienced. Make a list of the books, movies, comics, audio tapes, CD's, and websites that make you laugh. Then use them to put fun in your life.

- Look for the absurd and the silly. There is truth to the saying that "truth is stranger than fiction."

- Notice when you are taking yourself too seriously. Then read Coyote stories before you find yourself in one.

- Bring and invite humor into relationships, especially when there will be high stress such as a doctor's appointment, interactions with your healthcare insurance provider, or any situation involving authority figures. (Warning: Use extreme caution if going before a judge or the IRS.)

- Hang out with funny people—humor is contagious.

- Practice smiling—smiling is contagious.

- Get a laugh track—laughing is contagious.

- Start a journal, or if you journal already, make entries about what is funny in your life each day.

- Commit to having fun and exercising your sense of humor every day.

- Go to a magic store or a fun/novelty shop, get simple magic tricks, or learn to juggle. Buy a rubber clown nose; no one will know what to think of you!

- This one you have to make up on your own, so get to work, and be serious about your sense of humor.

- Remember, "If you are too busy to laugh, you are too busy." ~ Unknown

- Have fun!

LET THE GOOD TIMES ROLL
LET THEM KNOCK YOU AROUND
LET THE GOOD TIMES ROLL
LET THEM MAKE YOU A CLOWN
LET THEM LIFT YOU UP IN THE AIR
LET THEM BRUSH YOUR ROCK AND ROLL HAIR
LET THE GOOD TIMES ROLL

~ THE CARS, BY RIC OCASEK
1978 ELECTRA/ASYLUM RECORDS

About
Rick Garrison

Rick Garrison, R.N., has specialized in cardiac care for 14 years. His experience ranges from a busy clinic at a metropolitan heart center to a cardiac intensive care unit to cardiopulmonary rehabilitation. He has held a variety of roles including management, health / lifestyle educator, and intensive care nurse. Because of his experience, Rick has in-depth knowledge of what people go through before, during, and after an encounter as a patient in a hospital.

Rick is also a student and practitioner of the healing energy techniques of Reiki and Qigong. Over the past decade, Rick has led rituals and ceremonies for groups, and provides 2nd degree Reiki healing for individuals.

Rick believes that the complicated and emotionally charged issues in today's modern healthcare system require openness for true collaboration to take place. He has worked to help improve, maintain, and support respectful communications in the modern medical arena.

Rick's life mission is to bring the sacredness of healing into the current health care environment. He cares deeply about creating change in the healing and caring aspects of modern health care. He acknowledges that modern medicine has made incredible technological advances, and that it is "powerful medicine." However, he also sees that the medical technologies are being provided with little regard to their power being a special gift.

As the principal of Stone Circle Healing, Rick assists others in their healing journey. As a seeker of truth, he honors all things as sacred: Other people, the earth, the creator, and our selves. He writes and speaks the stories that awaken our spirit and bring balance and wholeness to heal the world.

To contact Rick, call 612-719-0420 or email rickgarrisonrn@att.net.

Healing Through Sound

By Lynn Bieber

Early one morning in 1971, I was in a deep meditative trance and, without warning suddenly started making sounds. How interesting! At the time it felt so extreme I did not mention it to anyone, not even to my close buddies that met several times a week to practice our intuitive skills. A year later I attended a presentation by Patricia Sun at the New Age Learning Center, Anthropos. Patricia makes sounds, and people feel better. The evening was delightful. Everyone was excited. I was especially excited because as Patricia demonstrated her remarkable talents, I realized, "That's what I am doing!" I now had a touchstone from which I could push out into the world on my own! I became braver, shared with my friends what had been occurring, and started practicing on them, other friends, family, and even some willing clients. This gift has grown and expanded over the years. All self-consciousness has evaporated. Full trust of the process has taken place and I willingly and easily step into the loving space of *Sound* and let myself go.

Healing with *Sound* is an ancient art. Aborigines in Australia "sing the world into existence." Many people today are re-discovering the power of the voice to heal. Research shows that the energetic structure of a person is actually changed—rearranged—as a result of specific sounds. Healing and wholeness can take place with ease and grace by combining the voice, natural intuitive abilities and loving intent.

Expressing thoughts, emotions, and bodily sensations with sound is natural for human beings. Observe young children as they learn to use their voice. As adults, however, much of our natural expression has often been shut down, turned off, or held in due to criticism, ridicule, and threats. Reopening these areas of expression, releasing these pent up sounds is therapeutic, liberating, and exhilarating.

The Sacredness of Sounding

Sounding is a sacred experience for me. I ground myself and request help and guidance from "All That Is." I then state the intention and ask that this *Sounding* be for the *highest good* of all concerned and I enter a very light trance state. In trance, I look for a symbol, what I call the *template* that represents the individual or organization. Sounds form that are in affinity with this template. Very often these beginning sounds are heavy, irregular, sometimes guttural. These sounds remove the negative thought forms, beliefs, and traumas that are no longer needed. Soon the sounds begin to change and move into a more melodic, pleasing form. The person's essence becomes clearer and stronger. Deep appreciation, gratitude, and awe fill me at the conclusion of any *Sounding*.

12 Strands of Power

There are 12 Strands of Power I sing to when *Sounding*. These 12 Strands of Power are connected to our DNA and, ultimately, our soul. We know that our cells contain our DNA. In mapping DNA, the scientific community has discovered that DNA change. They cannot explain *how* DNA changes, but they know it does. DNA can be damaged and can accumulate extra stuff. For example, we know chemical spills affect us and can lead to cancer, blood issues, etc. Those changes take place at the cellular level through vibrations.

Humans enjoy drumming and music. These sounds can affect us positively or aggravate us. We can feel vibrations. Clearly, sound affects us. Those effects go to the cellular level and beyond to the soul of the person. You can deliberately choose healing sounds that will clear energies not in affinity with you, and strengthen those that are. Let the DNA of your cells vibrate to the healing sounds described below and imagine the influence it can have on your life.

12 Songs

A brief description of the *Sounding Intentions for the Strands of Power* follows:

1. Welcome Home

The first and foremost strand is "Welcome Home." The first step in any *Sounding* activity, in this strand we say hello to the Spirit, the essence of the person. *Sounding* brings forth vibrations that inform and mirror the self, and recalls soul connections. This first step, by itself, can make a remarkable difference for a person.

The intention is to re-connect, to come home to *The All of Creation, The One*. The basic template of the person's essential nature is called forth. The Soul or Higher Self is invited to guide this venture. These forces are asked to hold us in a loving, spiritual embrace. The *Sounds* activate and ignite the person's knowing of their Divine Origin. We are reminded that we are Divine—An Ongoing Spirit. This process assists the return to purity of self, and invariably produces tears.

Ada is a woman in her late 50's who has asked me to **Sound** *her. She has an air of weariness about her and I sense a life of intense suffering and struggle. As I tune in to Ada's template, the* **Sounds** *begin to disassemble and dissolve dark, heavy energies that are surrounding her template. As these energies dissipate and disappear, Ada's template appears. It is tarnished and dull. As the* **Sounds** *continue to work with the template it becomes shiny and vibrant. I experience a sense of joy and delight, as Ada's template becomes dynamic and vital. The* **Sounding** *comes to a close. I open my eyes and look into Ada's eyes. They are wide and*

I see awe and wonder in her face as she searches for understanding of what has just happened.

2. Clearing and Aligning

Each person, family, or organization has a *template*, an original design or structure of essence that is with us from birth. It could be likened to the templates one works with on the computer. These templates often become cluttered and clouded by the beliefs and experiences one accumulates in life. My inner connection with this original template guides the experience.

As I "look" at the template, *Sounds* and images appear, clearing out debris, old patterns, and beliefs that are no longer useful. The *Sounds* that emerge tend to:

- assist the person in disconnecting from energies that do not serve them
- release old energies from the past, such as slights or hurts
- acknowledge other lifetimes
- mend any tears, rips
- dissolve "crud" or crustiness on the template
- align them with the original template
- expand the template, if needed
- bring the template into full alignment with the soul and the soul's purpose

*One day in my meditation, I checked into the template of a non-profit board I serve on. I was dumbfounded! It was based in scarcity and sacrifice. After I got over my initial shock, I acknowledged the energy and the good that had already taken place. Then through **Sounding** I asked my spiritual "helpers" to work with the template, and to upgrade it into abundance and ease. There was much joy and laughter as this re-structuring took place.*

When I was finished, I called the administrator of the program and told her what I had done. She thanked me and was pleased that I had done that. Within the next week the organization had increased their bank account by $7000. She publicly stated she felt it was the result of the energy work I had done. Whether or not that is so, what has taken place is a major shift in the organization's well being.

3. calling Forth The "Real" You

In this strand, the "real" you is invited to step forward. You are challenged to own the beauty and goodness of your being. The natural self rises out of the soul essence of a person. It is self-regulating, always learning and growing. It forms and reforms throughout various lifetimes and never loses its essence. *Sounding* creates the safety required for the divine nature to enter more fully into this reality. Being who you truly are is liberating and energizing. Through the owning of your divinity, your magnificence, you invite your *soul cluster* to support you in your emergence. You can consciously choose to strengthen the family genetics that are desirable, and weaken—sometimes totally disabling—the undesirable genetics.

*In February 2002, at a conference called The Feminine Face of Leadership, I led a workshop on **Sounding**. The 17 participants were excited and eager to take part. Each person's **Sounds** were different and distinct. As one woman said later, "Even though we didn't know these women, we got to see the purity of each person through the **Sounds** that represented them."*

*This large group **Sounding** brought an intense learning experience. We had been together for several days and there was one particular person that I experienced as intrusive and rude. When she stepped up to be **Sounded**, I wondered if I would be able to set aside my personal reactions and truly "see" this woman for who she was at the deepest level. Thankfully, I was able to bypass my limited view of her, open my heart, and see her greater* *being. My prejudices and judgments melted away as I saw and experienced her true essence through the **Sounding**. What a wonderful gift that confirmed and affirmed my faith in the ability of these energies to bypass my own areas of judgment.*

4. Releasing/Letting Go

As humans, we all have beliefs and life experiences that are burdensome and distracting. We also tend to collect other people's beliefs and emotions, often not realizing they are not our own. Acknowledging what is not ours and releasing it is important. Releasing what no longer serves us is a powerful experience. Old beliefs drop away, leaving fresh, new energies to work with. We all carry family energies and patterns. Releasing the old and embracing the new is a necessary step in our evolutionary journey. Releasing old self concepts and beliefs about ourselves that are untrue, divesting ourselves of old baggage, hurts, wounds, and lies is a critical step in personal and spiritual growth. It is a time to energetically release what no longer serves us.

*Dennis is a 50 year-old man who recently lost his job. As a result, he had been experiencing deep grief and a sense of profound failure. As we discussed his situation I saw that this was a repeat of the pattern he had in his relationship with his father. Through **Sounding** he was able to see the pattern more clearly, thank it for serving him so well, and then release it. He is now free to decide for himself what type of relationship he wants between him and the outer world. His countenance reflected the change—his eyes glowed, his face relaxed, his energy was renewed.*

5. Elevating and Stabilizing Energies

This strand fine-tunes, ignites, and strengthens the desirable vibrations. Shifting the energetic structure into the highest level possible increases their gifts and beauty. The *Sound* then tunes up and builds up the chords of joy, delight, and peace that reside in the cells of the body. The next step in the process is combining, grounding, and strengthening these energies with the earth and cosmic energies. Joining together, they flow throughout the body and the energy system, which appears as a bubble around the person. Working in unison with the Higher Self, the person is immersed in the most powerful range of energies possible for them at this time.

Mauricio and Mariana, a young couple with two children, are struggling to adapt to a foreign culture and a job that demands 10 to 14 hours a day plus weekends and evenings. The tensions and challenges of this situation often appear insurmountable. One of the gifts they have given themselves is meeting with me every two weeks to assist them in keeping their perspectives, plus a **Sounding** *that acknowledges who they are as spiritual beings. The stabilizing and elevating* **Sounds** *add strength to their decisions and commitments to their relationship and family. Each session begins with tensions and discontentment high on the list. At the end of the session both are relaxed, smiling, and peaceful. Always there is a grateful comment on the power of the* **Sounding** *to heal the troubled waters.*

6. Igniting Magnificence

Sounds call forth sparks of energy that activate the vibrations of magnificence. These hidden elements of magnificence are invited to come forth, be recognized, strengthened, and ignited. Any additional energies of magnificence that are now ready to enter the earth plane are called forth and connected.

About 10 years ago I decided to clarify for myself my personal purpose for coming on the planet this time. What I was given was a bit scary for me. I was told my purpose was to bring magnificence to the planet, to strengthen the magnificence that was already here, and to ignite the magnificence that was waiting to be ignited. Needless to say my brain was filled with all kinds of comments about this information. I finally decided I had asked the question, now I must accept the answer, even though I felt I

*was probably the wrong one to actually put it into physical form.
I examined my life, professionally and personally, and I found
that it was a true statement. That I was always looking for the
magnificence, the beauty and goodness of the person or situation.
This was simply a bigger and broader view of what I was already
doing.Today I offer seminars entitled "Natural Genius" in which
participants are **Sounded** and encouraged to step into their own
magnificence. The experience is one of depth and growth in the
personal and spiritual realms. This is an even greater refinement
of my work in magnificence.*

7. Co-Creators—Calling In Helpers

Our society is familiar with praying for the help of
angels and saints. In my Shamanic studies I have developed
relationships with many other forms of consciousness that
are eager to work with us in a collaborative manner. Some
of the most powerful journeys for me have involved animal
helpers. They are waiting for us to wake up and invite them
to take part in our lives. Coyote is one of my favorites. He
always travels with me and provides safety and comfort.
Another is a beautiful black panther. He keeps me company
and any time I do a healing, this great animal eats the
unwanted energies that fall away. He tells me he loves doing
this and that he is happy to be of assistance. It is through
the inner eye, the inner realms of knowing that they appear.
They are brave and wise. They can be very humorous and
they love to dance. In my training I was encouraged to
dance with my animals. There is such joy and celebration
in that activity.

One of the "natural laws" is that these other levels of
consciousness cannot help us unless they are invited. Their
integrity would not allow them to interfere with our lives.
We must consciously invite them to assist us or become
partners. Every culture has myths and tales of helpers from
other realms of consciousness. There are angels, fairies,
saints, animal spirits, power animals, archetypes, Gods and

Goddesses, and the Ultimate, "All That Is." We can invite them to join us, direct, support, guide, inform, companion, and play.

*After a two day **Sounding** Seminar in Southern California I had one of the most powerful and interesting experiences of my life. All night long I had communion with the most amazing apparitions. They were huge and looked like they could be ancient ancestors of the elephants. Words fail to describe the experience. It was expansive, loving, embracing, and amazing. I refer to them as the Great Beings that reside at the center of the earth. Occasionally they will appear when I work with a person. Often I call upon them to provide what is needed. We can and must ask for help. I believe this is much of the bounty of our existence. I always ask only for those in affinity with me and the person or persons I am working with.*

8. Joy, Laughter, Deep Play

Faerie laughter, joyful noise, belly laughs, group laughter, babies gurgling and cooing, children's laughter, birds, storms, water, waves, sounds of pleasure, angelic bells, tinkling sounds, squirrels, birds, dolphins, kittens, and puppies at play all are representative of these energies.

There are times when the sounds of joy and laughter erupt out of me as I tune in to a person. These are invariably folks that radiate playfulness. It is as if they are the recipients of a constantly flowing, bubbling stream of joy and laughter that permeates their being and their lives.

Some of these people are amazed when this is the basic *Sound* of their nature. Often they have had a life experiencing depression and sadness. As they re-connect with their true nature the depression and sadness begin to wane.

*Susan came to see me because she had been in therapy for years and wanted no more "therapizing," as she called it. As I observed Susan I could see a light and playful spirit. As I **Sounded** this aspect of her she laughed, danced, and giggled for a full 15* *minutes. When I told her I saw her basic nature as one of joyful play she was stunned. She responded, "That is hard to believe since most of my life I have fought with the desire to not even be here!" I said, "Yes, I can believe that. For a spirit that delights in play and laughter, this is a pretty hard place to come to, let alone live a life in. I can see how that would make you despair." As Susan has acknowledged her true nature of playfulness, she has expanded these gifts into her daily life. The heaviness and despair are slowly disappearing.*

9. Love

Loving and being loved is beyond words. However, I will do my best. As you read these words please remember the times in your life when you have experienced being loved, or loving someone fully. That will help you understand what I am describing in this section.

The *Sounds* that emerge at this time are what I call Heart Sounds. My own heart feels like it is filling until it overflows with love through the *Sounds*. A warm, enveloping energy surrounds us. Invariably tears of richness flow as I feel these powerful energies of appreciation, devotion, adoration, and pleasure. I have experienced these emotions in my own life upon the birth of our children. It is clear to me that love is the energy, or glue, that holds the entire cosmos together. There is purity and innocence present. Peace pervades the room, the kind of peace I experience when I am in Nature, far from the hustle and bustle of the everyday world. Fragments of this love come to us through our children, mates, friends, family members, pets, music, the arts, and nature.

Many years ago I worked with a woman named Celia. She was a bright, gentle creature faced with some serious challenges. Due to these challenges she shifted to working with a clinical psychologist. She received the help she was seeking and was grateful. However, one day she called and asked for an appointment. Puzzled, I agreed. As she settled into my office she *began to relax. I asked her why she had requested this appointment. She responded, "I needed to feel loved." The **Sounding** filled spaces within her that simple talk therapy could not touch. This always leaves me with a feeling of amazement and gratitude.*

10. Core Essence

The Core Essence is a column of energy that runs from below the feet to above the head. The basic structure of the unique self is expressed in this area. Closed areas open up as the *Sound* pours forth. Energies that are ready to be expressed and developed appear. The Core Essence is strengthened, renewed, cleared, and purified of energies that are not in full affinity with it. This Essence is closely associated with Natural Genius, that unique gift that only we bring to the world. Natural Genius is often a place where we judge others because it's "so simple anybody could do it!" At times we may have experienced criticism from those around us, often family members, and as a result we have shut down the expression of our unique gifts, our Natural Genius. As each of us steps fully into our Natural Genius the world will be a very different place.

*Susan, Gail, and Connie work together. One is a masseuse, another a chiropractor, another does acupressure, Jin Shin Jyutsu and Shiatsu. I met with them to explore how they could become more visible in the community and bring in more clients. As we talked, defining desires and expressing dreams, the excitement grew. **Sounding** each of these women was a real treat. The **Sounds** for each were distinctly different. Each person wrote and shared their experiences of their own **Sounding**, as well as the **Sounding** for the others. They ended up with a list of qualities for themselves. Gail saw and accepted that she is a visionary, loves to plan, organize, and create the structure for a bigger picture. Connie is fascinated with community and automatically builds community and outreach wherever she is. She realizes that she has done this all her life. Susan is recognized for her joy and delight in life itself. As they discussed these attributes they decided to "assign"* *each other these areas as their gift to the business. Together they created an altar and a small written statement of each person's purpose in the business. The number of clients has increased. Stability, inclusiveness, and joy permeate their office now.*

11. Soul Retrieval

Soul retrieval is a concept brought to us from the Shamanic traditions. It is a belief that when one experiences trauma, shock, pain, or disillusionment, a portion of the soul leaves and goes to a safe, comfortable place. In ancient times the Shaman recognized this and called these parts back in during the community rituals that were a common practice. Soul Retrieval can take place through *Sounding.*

Setting the intention of soul retrieval and inviting the soul parts to return as they are ready is the key. This includes inviting future aspects of the soul willing to join us now.

The practice of soul retrieval is returning. Jill Kuykendall has become well known for this ability. In her hospital-based physical therapy practice, she often observed a sudden shift in energy, and then the person would sigh and say, "That feels better!" She had observed this over the years and even reached the point where she waited for it and often invited it to occur. It was only much later that she learned about the Shamanic tradition of soul retrieval. Combining her experiences within the framework of soul retrieval was a powerful move for her and a blessing for those who receive her services.

Mariana, one of my clients, is attractive, bright, and committed to spiritual and personal growth. At the age of 2, her daughter, Amanda, had been having trouble sleeping at night, was often cranky during the day, and would often become inconsolable. Since this was not Amanda's normal way of being in the world, Mariana asked me to take a look at her psychically. The first picture I received was the "Love Sandwich," placing Amanda between Mariana and me and holding her. Then I was shown that Amanda's surgery experience when she was a one-

year-old had caused a piece of her soul to leave. My helpers sought this soul piece and returned it to me. I in turn gave it to Mariana by blowing the energy into her heart and the top of her head and directed her to do the same for Amanda.

The next week, her mother and father reported the following: Mariana said to Amanda, "I have a gift for you that will make you a happy person. Do you want it?" Amanda answered, "Yes." Her mother said, "It's in my heart." Mariana cupped her hands and with a deep breath blew "the gift" into Amanda's heart and head. The parents reported immediate and vast changes. Amanda slept 12 hours that first night—the first time she had ever done that. She was happier, more pleasant, and relaxed following this event.

12. Blessing

The final phase of any *Sounding* is a request for a blessing from the Divine Source. It is a time of overwhelming love and beauty. The vibrations of the Sounds are ethereal, intense, and beautiful. Tears of gratitude, appreciation, and wonder flow freely. It is a time of peace, oneness, and perfection.

The Evergreen Spiritual Community has asked me to give a blessing of **Sound** *to the gathering. There are a dozen of us forming a circle. As I tune into the energies and request a blessing from* **All That Is,** *I am surrounded by a warm, loving energy. My body relaxes and* **Sounds** *issue forth. The* **Sounds** *are beautiful, expansive, and relaxing. I am reminded of lullabies being sung to beloved children when the Soul of the Mother joins with the Soul of the Child. The ethereal* **Sounds** *continue and I feel the entire group is lifted up and held in a loving embrace. The* **Sounds** *are complete and we stand in silence, relishing the peace and beauty of the moment.*

Prayer, Intention, Gratitude, and Sound

The most important elements of *Sounding* are prayer, intention, gratitude, and the actual *Sounds*. Drums, masks, rattles, bells, and tuning forks add diversity and their own form of magic. Playful exploration is at the heart of successful healing.

Here is a simple process to help you experience the power of *Sound*. Allow yourself 10 to 30 minutes for each exercise. Do each exercise for two to seven days:

1. Listen to music that is uplifting and inspiring. Pay attention to any feelings and physical sensations that arise.

2. Combine listening to inspirational music with meditation and prayer. Take note of mental, physical, and emotional responses.

3. Meditate in silence with the focus on your soul. Center your awareness in your heart area. Allow any kind of sound that wants to emerge at this time. There is no right or wrong. Just make sounds. Write down your thoughts and feelings. Are you more relaxed? Happier? More thoughtful?

4. For physical or emotional discomfort, enter a meditative state. Focus on what is calling to you, give it a *Sound*, and continue *Sounding*. It will change and inevitably the sound will move into a pleasurable mode. A sense of relaxation will take place and you will know you have shifted energy within your body and moved into a healing or wholeness.

5. Find a friend or family member that you can trust and ask if you can experiment with sounding them. Explain the process and let them know you want feedback on the experience. Children are especially receptive to *Sounding*.

Sounding, so natural, so simple, so healing. We all know how to do it. In fact, we do it every day. Expanding this gift can bless our world in countless ways.

Suggested Readings

Dossey, Larry. *Healing Beyond the Body: Reinventing Medicine*; Shambala Publishing; www.dosseydossey.com.

Gaynor, Mitchell L., MD. *Sounds of Healing*; Broadway Books.

Gerber, Richard. *Vibrational Medicine*; Bear & Co.

Marx Hubbard, Barbara. *Conscious Evolution*; P.O. Box 4698, Santa Barbara, CA 93140.

Moyers, Bill. *Healing and The Mind*; Doubleday.

Pert, Candace, Ph.D. *Molecules of Emotion*; Simon and Schuster.

Talbot, Michael. *The Holographic Universe*; Harper Collins.

Wesselman, Hank. *SpiritWalker; MedicineMaker, VisionSeeker, The Journey to the Secret Garden; Spirit Medicine: Healing in the Sacred Realms* co-authored with his wife, Jill Kuykendall.

About
Lynn Bieber

Lynn Bieber, M.S., M.F.T., uses her innovative work as a transformative force in the world. Her unique channeling of sound and language calls forth the deepest beauty and spirit within the hearts of those who hear her. This gift that she calls *Sounding* is ancient and new, profound and fun, easy, yet very powerful. Hank Wesselman, author and Shamanic teacher has referred to her as "one of our elders."

Lynn and her husband, Stan, have been married more than 50 years, raised four children, and now are the proud grandparents of six grandchildren and one great granddaughter. In addition to her rich life experiences, Lynn draws on more than 30 years of experience as a family therapist, spiritual guide, and metaphysician. She calls upon her deep training and experience in Shamanism, sound healing, and subtle energy work to help others discover their own natural gifts and talents. "We are sound before we are matter; sound has powerful abilities to change systems."

Lynn has developed her own view of the psyche, which she refers to as The Natural Self. This approach incorporates the multiple levels of expressive powers we each possess. Her desire to see each person ignite the magnificence that resides within has been the driving force in her work. Lynn has been using Sounding as an Entrepreneurial Healer with individuals and small groups for many years and is now stepping forward to expand the scope of her powerful, transformative work.

Lynn presents retreats and workshops. Lynn and Alexis McKenna (see chapter on "The Healing Power of Solitude") offer a course based in Western Mysticism entitled, "Developing and Sustaining Your Personal Relationship with the Sacred." For more information call 925-484-5969 (Lynn) or 503-838-1040 (Alexis), or visit the website www.entrepreneurialhealer.com. Lynn and Alexis also offer joint readings entitled "Infinite Possibilities."

Lynn is the author of the "Safe New Driver Party," a manual that supports parents and teens through the difficult and challenging rite of passage—driving!

How Music Soothed My Soul, Kept Me Whole and Forever Preserved the Joy in My Heart

By Lisa C. Morgan

THE PRELUDE:
"THE TENDER LADY HAS SADNESS IN HER EYES
SHE SEES THE FALLEN HOPES, THE LONELINESS AND LIES
TELL ME, HAVE YOU SOMETHING TO EASE HER PAIN
WHY NOT BRING HER HAPPINESS AND PEACE AGAIN."
~ CRIS WILLIAMSON, THE TENDER LADY

March 30th, 2004: My mom died September 15, 2003. At present, I am writing a chapter for the book, *Sacred Healing*. I'm going to tell "what I have always known I have always known" about myself since childhood. For as long as I can remember, I have been on a quest—*On The Road To Find Out* (Cat Stevens). *Why, oh Why, oh Why?* (Anne Murray).

My story begins August 1951. I'm in utero in my mommy's belly. Although I've traveled *The Long and Winding Road* (Beatles), where I've ended up is where I first began—back in the loving embrace of my mother. However, it wasn't always that way. In truth, my mother and I shared many rough and rocky times. Only today can I honestly say that I feel her presence and love in my heart in a way that I was never *fully* able to experience in her lifetime. Although I feel that my entire life has been a journey on a spiritual path, nothing has been as sacred as the healing that has come to me through the connection with my mother and music. This is our story.

"The Music, My Mom and Me" Connection

September 7th 2003. The Hospital ICU—My Mother's Death Bed: My mother has been in intensive care for over a week and things are not looking good. She's been heavily sedated, on a respirator, and her body is retaining fluids. I'm feeling desperate to get home to see her, for more and more I am sensing it will be to say good-bye. I have two really important commitments to keep, and am praying to God for Mom to "please hang in there for me." When I arrive in Cincinnati I rush straight to the hospital. All I can think about is seeing my mother and singing to her. I'm not sure why it is so important. All I know is that I feel compelled to sing.

When I finally see my mother, I do a double take. She looks so much like my grandmother, and is blown up like the Pillsbury doughboy. With a sinking feeling inside, I sense her time may have come. After dissolving into tears, I rush to her bedside to hug and kiss her. After regaining my composure, I step back and ask my brothers and sisters-in-law if they would like to sing a song with me. I know they are completely taken aback by my request, but humor me nevertheless. They urge me to sing.

As I lay my head down next to my mother's ear, I softly start singing, "Let there be peace on earth and let it begin with me . . . With God as our father, family all are we . . . Let us walk with each other, in perfect harmony." As my brothers look on, I can not see what they see. Hours later they explain what happened. My mother's vitals were being closely monitored. Everything had been tracking at a steady pace, with her heartbeat at 80 beats per minute. Suddenly the monitors went wild and her heartbeat shot down from 80 to 0. My brothers stood in shock, fearing the worst: "That's it! Mom waited for Lisa and now she's gone." Eventually her heart started to beat again.

Months later I made sense of this episode. By writing this chapter many realizations have come to me. This "aha" was a Music Therapy connection. Back in the 1980's, as I researched ways to take Music Therapy hospital-wide, I read a case study about a Music Therapist who took a flute into an ICU to play for a patient who'd been comatose for weeks. When the patient eventually regained consciousness, the first thing she talked about was a flute.

Obviously, a "hearing" connection had been made. I believe it was this buried memory (an inkling from my subconscious) that triggered my urge to sing to my mother. As a Music Therapist, I know that hearing is the first sense to develop in utero and the last to go before dying. When I arrived in Cincinnati, all I wanted was to be able to make contact with my mother. Today, I feel blessed, knowing that she heard me. The machines were her way of communicating she knew I was there.

When we finally decided it was time to let my mother go, I had another compelling urge. First, *all* of her loved ones *had to be present* when she died. Second, I insisted there *had to be music*. My brothers and I returned to her apartment to look for some tapes. I was on a mission to find just the right music. I found it in her bedroom—two tapes of solo piano by Collin Redfern. I knew if they were there, she had listened to them often. Besides, Mom and I both played the piano, so I knew these would be *perfect*!

Approximately an hour after disconnecting the respirator, my mother's heart stopped beating. Each of us took turns hugging, stroking, and kissing her, as well as embracing one another while swaying to the music of the melodies we knew so well. When it was over, Mom took her last breath and peacefully passed on. She was surrounded by everything that mattered most to her—her children, her adorable new husband, and the sound of music. She blessed us all with the gift of her passing in our presence.

The Weeks After the Memorial Service

The memorial service and reception were magnificent. We had piano music at both. In writing her eulogy, I had another *huge* epiphany. Although I'd always known I shared many of the same interests as my mother, I'd never quite put the big picture together as it came to me then. I realized my mother's influence on *everything* that meant *anything* to me in life, especially my connection to music and the piano.

At the reception, I felt such joy to reconnect with so many of my mother's life-long friends—especially the women. They spoke so lovingly about what they would miss most—all the fun they had shared, especially the giggling as only girlfriends can do. At the time I felt soothed and uplifted by their stories. By the time I returned home, extreme anguish and torment overtook me. My body ached from the inside out, with an intense physical pain that was all consuming. No matter what I did, I couldn't shake it. My anguish came from the mental comparisons of my *memories* of mom juxtaposed with my *imagined* hearing of her laughter and giggling with her friends. Though *they* had shared much fun, all I could hear inside my head were her *tormented sounds*—my memories from my childhood and teen years. It felt like a living nightmare, and my body hurt.

How the Sounds Live on Inside of Us

"THE MEETING OF TWO PERSONALITIES IS LIKE THE CONTACT OF TWO CHEMICAL SUBSTANCES: IF THERE IS A REACTION, BOTH ARE TRANSFORMED." ~ CARL JUNG

My connection to my mother's voice, to her provocative sounds, and to the physical and emotional agitation in her body, began for me as a fetus in her womb. I know because of the work I've done in Bioenergetic Therapy, as well as from information she shared several years before dying. What was living inside of me has surfaced and is now recorded on tape. In listening to sections of these tapes, one might imagine hearing a conversation between a mother and very small baby (or fetus immersed in amniotic fluid), for there are two distinct voices, responding to one another in distress.

Research proves that the unborn child first senses sound vibrations through the body (muscles, skin, bones) and later listens/hears through the ear. According to Dr. Alfred

Tomatis, the ear is "the Rome of the body"—almost all cranial nerves lead to it. The electrical charge of sound stimulates the brain to grow. And sound provides the first vehicle for making contact with a fetus. By week 16, a fetus responds to sound pulses in specific ways, even though the ear is not fully developed. Ultrasound scans show babies covering their ears to block out loud noises. Unborn babies are known to habituate to, learn from, and think about what they hear. "Familiarization with specific sounds before birth may induce a special sensitivity to, recognition of, and even preference for those sounds after birth." (*The Mozart Effect For Children*, by Don Campbell)

The charged sounds *and* physical sensations (wracking, heaving sobs) during my last five months of gestation, became indelibly imprinted upon my brain and body in the womb. I became hard-wired, so to speak, to be keenly attuned to sound, especially my mother's sounds.

Bioenergetics:
Our Bodies as a History of our Biography

"THAT WHICH IS WITHIN YOU AND EXPRESSED WILL SET YOU FREE. THAT WHICH IS WITHIN YOU AND NOT EXPRESSED WILL EAT YOU FROM THE INSIDE." ~ AUTHOR UNKNOWN

In 1996, I became very interested in Bioenergetic Therapy because of a profound experience I had in a workshop entitled, *Finding Your Voice*. I knew I wanted to pursue more work in this method because of the parallels I saw between Bioenergetics and Music Therapy, both of which access energy, sound, voice, and body in their healing work. As synchronicity would have it, I made an appointment for my first session a week before my mother died.

Initially, I thought I was there to heal my love/hate relationship with my voice. For years I'd known that I carried an internal resistance to singing, especially in public—something that created much angst for me as a

Music Therapist. Ever since childhood, I'd known that something had a grip on my voice. I remembered how I had played with my dolls in my childhood bedroom, first in a speaking voice, then a whisper, and finally in silence. I wondered why. I had my theories, but it wasn't until the Bioenergetics workshop that I had my first clue.

> "YOUR VOICE IS A SOURCE OF STRENGTH, A WAY OF ASSERTING YOUR ALIVENESS AND YOUR RIGHT TO BE THAT WHICH YOU ARE. EVEN MORE DEEPLY, YOUR VOICE IS YOU, YOUR IDIOM, A UNIQUE EXPRESSION OF WHO AND WHAT YOU ARE IN THE WORLD. MANY OF US ARE TAUGHT NOT TO HAVE OUR VOICE. THERE ARE MANY REASONS, AND SOME ARE VERY COMPELLING. BUT IT HAS TREMENDOUS COST. WE BECOME WOLVES WITHOUT A HOWL, LIONS WITHOUT A ROAR, AND SONGBIRDS WITHOUT A SONG—VULNERABLE TO DEPRESSION AND IMPOTENT RAGE." ~ JOHN MAY, PH.D

Bioenergetics purports that our body is our biography, meaning we store the unexpressed and repressed feelings from our past within. Feelings are emotions (energy in motion), but if they become blocked or trapped, can become toxic (like stagnant water). Bioenergetics puts one's body into stress positions (to make the muscles quiver), while voicing sound (ahhhh). This process helps force a flow of energy that can help break through one's internal tensions (armor) that hold things in. Think of the African dancers who gyrate and vibrate for hours on end. They are pure energy in motion. We are no different. Without our internal blocks, we could have access to this endless stream of energy, for energy is all that we are (Quantum Physics). Voicing one's natural sounds provides the key to accessing and releasing repressed emotions. Before man ever had language, he communicated his needs and wants through sounds (grunts, groans, cries, yells, etc.). The same is true for babies. Body/voice work is important to breaking through energy blocks that hold everything in.

In pursuing the Bioenergetics, I hoped to feel free to access the delight of singing, as only a child can do. When the student is ready, the teacher appears. A higher power was guiding me toward another opening for a deeper healing.

When I first started the process, I had no clue what sounds to expect. During my initial body scan (my therapist looking at me in a bathing suit), I learned that I had trapped energy in my midriff. She also noted much tension in my jaw (I've recently completed major dental work on teeth worn down to the gums); eyes recessed way back in the sockets (what was I afraid to see as a child?); and the energy in my legs pulling up (as if I weren't firmly grounded). Interestingly, I have samples of drawings I've made that consistently show stick figures of myself without feet.

The catharsis I've experienced in this work has been astounding and magical. I've been amazed by the results I've achieved, especially the sense of completion. Music Therapy and Coaching have contributed much to my ability to synthesize the revelations into a cogent whole that makes sense for me. Bioenergetics calls this reintegration process "self possession." I call it "putting the puzzle pieces of my life back together" in a way that brings much inner peace and wholeness.

Three months into the process, I achieved a full body vibration. Although I had only had little tastes of success along the way, I trusted the process. I knew if I continued to ask myself the provocative questions for the answers I sought, they would eventually surface through my subconscious and intuition. I've never been afraid to ask the hard questions, nor to look truth in the face with brutal honesty, even when it exposes my ugliness, imperfections, and mistakes. Each revelation brings me to a deeper level of knowing, self-acceptance, compassion, forgiveness, and self-love. And the answers always seem to come just at the right time—when I am ready to receive and hear them. We *all* have the answers we seek inside of us.

When the breakthroughs came, they were a *huge* surprise. The only way to describe what happened was as if a lid had been removed from the top of a well—deep within the core of my being. A huge surge of energy poured forth with sound erupting like a volcano. As the sensation grew, my jaw dropped open wide (like a snake disconnecting its joints at the mouth). Screams of terror came spewing forth. I was absolutely astonished. As fast as it started, it stopped and I was spent. Initially it was only the "terror" sounds that appeared; eventually many more would surface.

To hear my sounds on tape, you might think you were listening to a horror movie. There are screams of terror and the strangled, snarling growls of a caged cat. It's amazing how my body instinctively modulates to accommodate and produce the sounds. There's been everything from a tightly constricted throat to the coughing, choking, and heaving sensations in my chest and abdomen. I never forced anything, but allowed what would be to be. The most startling sound emerged like the soft, muffled mews of a baby kitten that had lost its mother. Eventually these changed to a high-pitched, piercing babbling—"bibibi-ing" and "bababa-ing," which became very agitated. My mother had told me about the grief and emotional trauma she experienced during her pregnancy with me. I have no doubt that these sounds were my fetus-self reacting to her distress. The heaving, sobbing sensations were her body's responses to her anguish and I absorbed them into my body like a sponge.

The juxtaposition of my childhood bedroom, the one closest to my parents' bedroom, meant I would continue to hear my mother's sounds (behind closed doors) throughout my childhood. I've always known that I heard my parents fighting, but I never realized how *deeply* frightening and unsettling these episodes were to my child self.

Thankfully, God also gave me an ear for music and a body that loves to move (especially to R&B, Motown, and funk!). My love of music provided me with healthy outlets and ways to keep my heart intact. As a child, words in music were never important. I only heard the sounds of the instruments, the melodies, harmonies, and rhythm. When I became a Music Therapist I had to force myself to listen to lyrics. Until then, words could be poison, especially if they were emotionally charged and destructive. Words tore my parents apart and pierced my heart. The sounds of music are what soothed, comforted, uplifted, and inspired me. My being drawn to music makes so much sense. For me, music was a magnet and manna from heaven—my source of solace and inspiration—a gift from God that protected and preserved the joy in my heart.

The Sacred Path, The Sacred Journey, The Most Sacred Healing

"THE BASIC PROBLEM OF ALL EXISTENCE, THE ROOT CAUSE OF ALL HUMAN SUFFERING, IS ALIENATION FROM THE MOTHER. SHE WAS THE WHOLE WORLD TO US—THE SOURCE OF ALL LOVE AND THE CAUSE OF ALL DISTRESS. RECONCILIATION WITH HER, THE GRATEFUL REUNION, IS THE TASK OF LIFE. THIS IS THE WAY, THE ONLY WAY, TO LOVE AND ENLIGHTENMENT."
~DR. JOHN DIAMOND, M.D., THE WAY OF THE PULSE

So where does this leave me? What profound connections have I made? I carry inside of me an extreme sense of rightness about who I am and always have been, especially as a Music Therapist and Coach. Both are my passions and have given me a profound sense of purpose and fulfillment. Both have contributed significantly to the healing that has reunited me with my mother. For this *is* the story of the mending of a heart, of a little girl who adored her parents—whose heart was being ripped apart by their unhappiness. No matter what age, a child never stops grieving the loss of their parents.

Although difficult to describe, healing is definitely a physical sensation in the body. It happens when one's present day adult consciousness unites with the body, mind, and heart sensations of the child-self within. As I reconnected with the intense body sensations of my mother's anguish, I also felt the grief of my inner child's heart. Although I cried much, my adult heart opened up. All of my inner tensions melted away and I became flooded with huge sensations of love and compassion for my mother. My heart felt light and free. Eventually I would come to a place within where I could finally release my mother's pain completely.

Later, I had another epiphany that helped me make sense of how these experiences may have affected the dynamics of my relationship with my mom while she was alive. I could see how my unconscious need to protect my child-self unknowingly spurred me on to keep my mother an arm's distance away to prevent taking in any more of her unhappiness. I had already internalized much of her pain and any more of it might have destroyed me. I now know that one of the safest ways to allow her in was through music—especially her piano playing. This too was an amazing "aha" that came through reflecting about this chapter.

I'd been wondering why I didn't have distinct memories of myself as a child playing the piano in my childhood living room—the place where I'd spent hours practicing. As I listened to Mom's Collin Redfern tapes, I had the realization. A simple embellishment stopped me short. I thought, "That could have been my mother playing!" Then I knew—this was why she liked him. He played the way she aspired to play. Although he was a professional, my mom had been a fine pianist. Then it hit me. I didn't remember *my* piano playing. I remembered *hers*. I loved to listen to her play. Instantly, I was transported back in time, body, and mind to the physical sensations of love and inspiration of my child-self within. Her piano playing touched, moved, and inspired me, and filled my heart with love.

"AND OF EVERYTHING ON EARTH, MUSIC CAN MOST REMIND US OF
HER (MOTHER) LOVE, AND HER INTENTION TO LOVE—FOR IT CAME
FROM HER, HER AT HER PUREST, HER MOST PERFECT—THE
PULSATION OF HER BODY, HER ROCKING, HER LILT, AND HER LULLABY.
A DRUM TAKES US BACK TO THE WOMB, TO THE WORLD OF
RHYTHM—HER RHYTHM—THE PULSATION OF HER HEART."
~ DR. JOHN DIAMOND, M.D., THE WAY OF THE PULSE

The painful auditory memories of my mom are finally dissipating. Once again, I'm in touch with positive images of a cute, adorable, loving little lady, laughing and giggling her way through an evening, especially the night of her wedding reception to her life-long friend and a dear, dear man.

My Definition of Music as Therapy

For all the years I've spent explaining music therapy, this is what *I now know unequivocally.* For me, music has always been my healing agent—the active ingredient that assuaged the inner angst and provided catharsis. The energy of music resonates and brings me to the place I need to be, whether it's introspection, comfort, or joy. The gutsy, funky, energetic rhythms of pop/rock, funk, blues, or jazz are my natural uppers—the feel-good vibrations that keep me happy.

My chosen path of Music Therapy was God's gift to me, for it kept me engaged in conversations in music and on my personal path to healing. I approached my work with the mindset that "if it worked for me, it might work for others." I used myself as a guinea pig—a living laboratory in which to try out new ideas for ways to employ my tool called music. In hindsight, it's fascinating to see how my two favorite programs—my sessions on *The Child Within* and the *Music Therapy Assisted Childbirth Program*—both teach how to protect and preserve the heart of the child within. Today, my *Music FUN Shops* help adults reconnect with their childlike spirit to bring love and joy back to the forefront of one's life.

Music as a Projection and Reflection of You

Most people intuitively understand music as therapy, but little do they truly understand how profoundly music impacts us on the physical/emotional/spiritual level. Research is proving this more and more. The impact has to do with Quantum Physics, music as a form of sonic energy whose vibrations impact the human energy system. Perhaps the study, "The Effect of Music and Multimodal Stimulation on Response of Premature Infants in Neonatal Intensive Care" (Pediatric Nursing), says it best: "... premature infants who received 15-30 minute sessions of Brahms Lullaby one or two times per week ... the music significantly increased weight gain for males and females and decreased females' days to discharge." Infants who received the prescribed doses of music gained weight faster and were discharged sooner than those who didn't. For these preemies, it was a matter of life and death; music played a vital role in giving them a better chance for survival.

Unfortunately, adults lose touch with what babies and children know to be true about music. I hope some day we will all return to knowing the power of music as it has been known through centuries. The Chinese character for medicine is the same as music. The Greek God Apollo was both the God of Medicine and Music. Ancient Greek philosophers Pythagoras and Plato knew that the right sounds (rhythm, melody, and harmony) played at the right time, by the right instruments, have the ability to provide a body/mind attunement, bringing all energy systems back to homeostasis, an inner state of harmony, balance, and equilibrium. As a Music Therapist / Coach it's my hope that we will get back to using music consciously, respectfully, responsibly, and intentionally for our highest good.

Even the Word "Music" is Music to My Ears

"In every note there is hope; in every musical phrase there is healing; and in every song, joy. Music offers a solution to every person; perhaps for every illness too."
~ Cathy Kunkel

Think of something you *really* detest. Got it? Spend a few minutes thinking about it. Now stop and listen. What do you hear inside your body/mind? Are you having any physical/emotional sensations? Can you feel the adrenaline pumping, your heart racing, or your breath becoming labored? Do you feel tension in your neck or shoulders? Try the same exercise with something you love. Give it a minute; then take another body scan. Are there any changes? Are you in touch with any feel-good sensations?

For me, just thinking the word "music" produces a real sensation of inner peace in my body/mind. It is a knowing that I carry within me that gives me access to this magic potion—a secret ingredient that keeps me feeling physically healthy, spiritually wealthy, and emotionally wise. Music has always revealed to me deeper levels of myself, and provided access to buried memories or openings within my subconscious. Because I am so keenly tuned into the healing vibration of music, it readily brings me back to a state of equilibrium and inner harmony.

I hope you will feel inspired by my story to begin to tune into music with a new intention to use music purposefully, for your highest good. Try writing in your journal about a time or event in your life when music made a profound and positive contribution. What did the music do for you? How did it meet your needs, address your wants, or mirror back to you aspects of yourself that sought validation, support, or solace? How does re-connecting with this positive memory make you feel right now?

Here are some questions to guide you further in exploring your personal relationship to music. Who knows what surprises you may encounter? Be sure to have fun with the process and tune into your music along the way!

- What kinds of music do you listen to the most? What do your current tastes say about who you are or what you need or want in your life right now? Do your choices reveal parts of your self or personality?

- Think about the musical "seasons" of your life. What stages have you been through? Have your tastes changed? What attracts you to a particular genre of music? Does it match or reflect your attitudes and beliefs? What do your current tastes say about how you have changed or grown?

- Do you ever use music "consciously" for specific reasons, at specific times? Try making a "Power" tape, a collection of songs to listen to when you want to feel relaxed, positive, empowered, motivated, or inspired.

- Schedule a music fun day. Visit a music store and see which CD cover and song titles attract you. Try listening to some new genres. Who knows what magic or mystery may open up through the power of music!

THE POSTLUDE:
"MUSIC, OH SWEET MEL-O-DY;
WON'T ... YOU DRAW .... HER ...CLOSE ...TO YOU;
AND COMFORT HER ... YES COMFORT HER
PLEASE COMFORT HER FOR ME!"
~ CRIS WILLIAMSON, TENDER LADY

June 1971: The year has been bittersweet—a great year at college intermixed with the turmoil of my parents' divorce. Both have remarried and I'm returning home for the summer. I don't quite know what to expect. My dad and stepmother are trying to encourage me by telling me I'll have the biggest bedroom in their house. Indeed it's huge, very long and rectangular. As my eyes travel the length of the room, I take in a most welcome sight—my baby grand piano. As I feel my body relax, my heart lifts. I know everything will be okay. My tried and true Rock of Gibraltar is there to greet me, ground me, and welcome me home. Little do I know how prophetic these thoughts will become. Where I was then, is where I have now come full circle again—back home to me—through the "music, my mom, and me" connection.

Even though I can no longer hug or kiss my mom, nor tell her in person what she means to me, I carry her presence in my heart forever—a permanent bond that was forged in the womb. The highly charged soundscape of her womb caused me to become so sensitive to sound. But it was through the sharing of her passion—the piano—that I received the gift of music in my life.

Thank you Mom, for your eternal gift of love and inspiration, for our eternal bond and connection through music, a connection that has forever preserved the joy in the heart and the spirit of love and exuberance that has always blessed and fueled my life! I miss you!

About
Lisa C. Morgan

Lisa C. Morgan, C.P.C., M.T.-B.C., combines over 25 years experience as a Board Certified Music Therapist with her experience as a certified professional coach, helping people to reconnect with their "authentic" voice, march to the beat of their own drum, and create a life that makes their heart sing!

Lisa is a Personal and Professional Life Strategy Coach with certification from International Coach Academy of Sydney, Australia.

Lisa believes that we have all been placed on this earth to discover our own true path and special gift from within. We will never truly be happy with our lives until we wholeheartedly (consciously) reclaim and integrate our true essence into all aspects of our life, both personally and professionally. When we are able to respond to the call of our soul and lead with our hearts, we can reclaim our personal power and gain clarity to focus a vision for our lives.

In 1980, Lisa began pioneering Music Therapy services in the general hospital setting in St. Louis. She specialized in the areas of personal growth and development, wellness, pain management, relaxation training, fitness, re-motivation, and leisure awareness, and was the first to bring Music Therapy Assisted Childbirth to St. Louis area hospitals. Her entrée into the field of coaching is a natural extension of passion for personal development and group work in the field of Music Therapy. Starting in 1995, she completed three intensive, transformative programs with

Landmark Education: the Forum, The Forum In Action, and The Advanced Forum.

Currently, Lisa owns and operates two businesses, Music Wellness Works, LLC and Fine-Tuning Your Life Coaching. She provides individual and group coaching services as well as music coaching presentations for personal health and wellness, quality of life, motivation, improved performance and success. She recently completed her training as a drum circle facilitator from "Health Rhythms" (Remo Drums). Lisa is an "experiential" group facilitator and is especially partial to her "Music Funshops," which tap into the positive energy of music to prevent burnout and promote resilience in individuals and teams in the corporate setting.

To contact Lisa, call 314-567-6176 or email LisaMusicWorks@aol.com.

A Guide's "Tail"

By Beth Kopitzke

Up in the mountain highlands there is a lush green valley, a magical place where animals, Humans, and angels reside in peace and speak with each other. On this day, six animals—two zebras, a red fox, a white Bengal tiger, a white filial fox, and a red panda—have come together to review the adventures of the Human, Beth.

"This has been quite the year for Beth, hasn't it?" asked the tiger, Star.

"That it has been," agreed Zen and Thai, the zebras.

"Aidian, since you've known Beth the longest, please tell us about what her life was like before, so we can understand what the changes she is making mean to her," asked Pandy, the red panda.

Filly, the filial fox chimed in, "Yes, please Aidian, do tell."

Aidian, the red fox, made himself comfortable for the telling of this tale. "When I came into Beth's conscious life a few years ago, she was just starting to get her bearings."

"Bearings? What are bearings?" inquired Filly, who, being the youngest, didn't always understand Human language.

Star chuckled as he replied, "Bearings in Human context can either refer to metal balls used in their machinery, or in Beth's case, her outlook on her life, to figure out where and who she is and where she is going."

Filly nodded her head in understanding, turned and said, "I'm sorry I interrupted, Aidian. Please continue."

"As I was saying, Beth was getting her bearings. She realized many years ago that she was here on Earth for a reason, even though she had not found her purpose yet. Humans have this concept of Heaven and Hell, and some even realize that living on this planet is the Hell that their religions talk about. Beth had been to the depths of those nine nether Hells twice, attempting to kill herself at the ages of 13 and 31. The first time she tried, her body rejected the pills and alcohol she used. The second time, another soul reached out, sending her an email at just the right moment to help her realize she wasn't alone." Aidian paused, reflecting on that moment. "Beth wasn't aware of me at that time. I knew there was more for her to do. But in the depths of her exhaustion and depression, she couldn't see anything but the darkness. The email from that soul gave her just enough light to see there was something inside she had to fulfill."

"Wasn't it at that point . . ." asked Zen.

". . . When she got help with the chemical imbalance in her brain?" finished Thai.

"Yes," Aidian replied. "That was when she sought medical help for the depression she has fought all her life. The medication helped balance things in her brain, until her brain learned how to make changes at the neurological level so she didn't need the medication any more."

"How did she learn to change her neurology?" Pandy asked.

"Fast forward four years to about 17 months ago," Star said. "That's where she really takes off."

Aidian picked up the story. "Beth's mom, Lil, died on August 2, 2002. Beth knew it was coming, just not when. When she recalled the night before Lil died, she realized that her intuition had been telling her to call Lil. She didn't, and the next morning she got the call at work to come home. By the time she arrived, Lil's spirit had already left her body. Beth stayed with Lil until the shell let go. Watching her mom die hit Beth harder than she realized, even though she'd been preparing for years for that moment. Her mother's death made her realize she has a lot of work to do before her shell expires."

"Didn't Beth's dad's spirit tell her what was to come?" asked Filly.

"He did, as much as a spirit can when speaking through someone else," answered Aidian. "In November of that year, Beth went to see an Intuitive, a Human who recognizes and uses the talents they have to remain connected to us spirit guides, the angels, and what Humans call their unconscious and higher conscious minds. The Intuitive did a process called Ho'oponono to help Beth let go of the energy cords she has to the people in her life. All of the cords let go but one—to her dad. He told the Intuitive to tell Beth that he loved her, he apologized for his behavior while he was alive, and asked if he could go with her on the 13 month journey she was about to take."

"Beth didn't understand the 13 month journey stuff, did she?" asked Filly.

"No, she had no idea of what was about to happen," Aidian replied. "The Intuitive told her about a school called The Meta Institute and their therapeutic coaching class that might be in line with the ideas Beth had about becoming a Personal Life Coach."

As Star rolled and stretched, he said, "Ya know, if Beth had had any inkling about the stretch and transformation she was inviting into her life, she probably wouldn't have made the leap. She trusted enough to let the Universe provide for her. Now, if we could only get her to trust other things…"

Aidian smiled, as only a fox can, replying, "We know what the Universe has planned. She does trust. She has just learned to be very careful and specific with her wishes. As it was, she let the idea of the Meta Institute go until just before Christmas, when she looked up the website and contacted them. That step was the first in the rest of her journey. Of course, she was admitted to the school, being the bright, wonderful woman we all know she is.

"The first weekend of class for her broke everything loose. When she asked about genetic depression, her instructors told her that depression is a choice. She could choose to continue being depressed or she could choose to hand the depression back to the previous generations and be free. I found it quite humorous to watch her face as that idea sank in. Her neurology started to change, and she got the internal headache that she now associates with her neurons changing pathways and her release of the genetic depression."

"Changing how she thought at the neurological level freed up the energy she would need to make the transformations to come, right?" Pandy asked.

"That it did, Pandy. That it did," Aidian said.

"Okay, now, wasn't it in class that her dad showed up again?" Filly asked. "Didn't she wonder if she actually 'saw' him to her left?"

"That's correct, Filly," Aidian replied. "One of the assistants for class was an Intuitive, so Beth asked. The assistant told Beth she was seeing correctly, and through the assistant, her dad asked if he could stay in class so he could learn what he didn't while he was alive. She was surprised at this request, and gave her assent."

"Beth's real awareness of her talents surfaced that day . . ." Thai began to say.

". . . And her healing gift began to manifest as well," Zen concluded.

"Beth has always known of her talents, she just didn't know where or how to put them to use in her life's purpose," Star commented.

"So when did her conscious mind catch up with her unconscious about the healing?" Filly questioned.

"Patience, little one," Aidian said. "I'm getting there. The first weekend went by quickly, as did the second and third. She learned about neuro-linguistic programming, or NLP, and how the language a person talks about their problems or issues with is the same language that is used to un-do the problem. Learning that the problems are outcomes that no longer serve her opened doors to how she could change the way she looked at her past. Knowing everything in life happens for a reason is one thing. Understanding how to change an event's impact through her current awareness changed how she looked at her life. She didn't have to be trapped in looking at her parents through the eyes of a frightened child. She could choose to look at them through the compassionate eyes of an adult who understands that they did the best they knew how, and that she chose them as parents to get the lessons she needed to step into her roll as a healer in this lifetime."

"April, an appropriate time for things to bloom, was when Beth took her Reiki classes," Star said, turning to Filly. "That was when she began to feel how the healing flowed through her hands."

"So, she needed a structure first," Filly said. "Then when she finally felt the energy flow, that's when she made the connection."

"Correct," Star replied. "That's when she made the leap and started to claim her purpose. However, there were still a few loose ends that she needed to weave in before her path would become clear."

"That's right, Star," Aidian said. "Several years ago Beth had taken classes to become a massage therapist. She loved the idea of helping people with touch. She had no awareness of how touch, combined with her intuitive skills, could help people. One day she massaged a young woman, and Beth knew the woman had been raped. Her training had not given her the skills to even broach the subject. Soon after, Beth shut down her massage practice and went the corporate route, which led her to the place of exhaustion.

"During the summer, as she learned more about NLP, and the beginning of Ericksonian hypnosis, she had the opportunity to exchange massage therapy for energy work with others in the area. She began to realize what a powerful combination of skills she had, with the massage therapy to work out the 'issues in the tissues,' the therapeutic coaching to help process those issues as they come up, and the energy work to help the seen and unseen body heal."

"That's when the Universe 'flowed' on her . . ." Thai started.

". . . And she was ready to 'flow' with it," Zen finished.

"The two-as-one can be puny and profound, eh?" Star chuckled.

"Well, she did go with the flow the universe provided," Aidian said. "After she quit her job, she started cleaning her house. She had been saying for months she needed to clean, but the Universe got tired of hearing her say it, and provided the water necessary to make things move. The dishwasher hose two floors above broke that July morning to get her moving. Between the mold and the mess, the cleaning in all areas of her life began. The physical boxes of stuff from her mom's house were sorted, donated, or thrown. The memories of the physical were dealt with as well. As she transformed, so did her living space. Instead of living in someone else's life, she began living in her own. The paint, cabinets, and flooring were exterior examples of what was happening inside."

"So what happened when she got her living space all fixed up?" Filly asked. "Is Beth all fixed up inside as well?"

"Filly, Humans can take their entire lifetimes to fix, as you say, their insides," Aidian replied. "Beth believes that she has chosen to take on a Human body many times, so her soul can work through the many things she needs to learn before she can ascend to the next level of being."

Filly and Pandy looked at Aidian, their confusion showing on their faces. "You mean that Beth will continue to 'peel the layers,' as she says, until she has worked through all her issues in this lifetime, and she still won't be done?" Pandy asked.

"Yes," Aidian replied. "She will work on the various issues throughout her current lifetime, and there will still be issues to work on when she chooses her next Human body."

"That seems stupid," Filly concluded. "You keep coming back until you get it right?"

"From your perspective, Filly, that is true for you," Aidian said. "Beth's map of reality, based on what she has experienced in this lifetime, is true for her now. She may learn something in the future that will change her beliefs and values and her map about how her soul works."

Everyone took a few moments to contemplate those thoughts.

"Humans are much more complex. . ." Thai said.

". . .Than they can even began to recognize," Zen replied.

"Just as we," Thai continued, indicating himself and his mate Zen, "represent Beth's duality of warrior and healer on this plane of existence . . ."

". . . She has the warrior and healer in her reality," Zen finished.

"That's right," Aidian said. "She chose this lifetime to manifest healing, and to put away her warrior side. Her warrior side manifested as an armor of obesity.

"When Beth was a child, her parents were rarely there for her. They didn't know how to give her unconditional love and the energy a child needs to become a whole Human. She turned to the only other energy source she knew was readily available—food. As she comes into awareness and makes the connections, she will integrate the healer and warrior so the armor of obesity can fall away."

"Aren't healers usually loners, and don't need other people in their lives?" Filly asked. "Looking at Beth's life, she seems to always be alone."

"Until now, that was the case for Beth," Star replied. "She used her armor to keep others away. Some saw through it and befriended her. If you are thinking mate-wise that she has been alone, that is true. As a healer, she must draw from masculine and feminine energies. She has to balance those inside, so she is whole on her own, before her mate can come forward."

"So, is there a mate out there for her?" Filly asked. "She's been through so much, and that's the one place in her life that seems so incomplete."

"There is a mate waiting for her," Star said. "She has a few more things to work through inside. When those issues are taken care of, he will be there."

"Good," Filly replied. "I want her to be happy, loving, and joyful."

"We seem to have gone off on a tangent," Aidian stated. "A relevant tangent, but a tangent none-the-less. As Beth worked through the months of class, her living space got closer to what she wanted. She continued to work on the issues and illusions in her life, to read and make connections. The hypnosis she experienced in class allowed many things she didn't need to be swept away, and the energy work helped her integrate the changes into her life."

"Wasn't it during the fall that a storm swept into her life?" Filly asked. "One of those you know in your gut, you feel in your heart, yet you have no physical proof of its existence?"

"Ah, that storm of emotion and illusion, that results in some very real consequences," Aidian said. "Beth felt the storm forming around people she cared about, and looking back she saw the pieces fall into place. She was not directly in the storm's path. Yet, like a real tornado that levels one side of a street and leaves the other side unscathed, debris falls for miles. For Beth, the debris in this storm caused her to fluctuate between illusion and reality. The reality was that the storm changed her relationships with those in and connected to the storm. The illusion was created to shield her from what was going on."

"The choices she made based on the illusion were what hurt her," Star explained. "Her logical, conscious brain told her one thing; her heart and intuition told her the truth. For whatever reason, she followed her conscious brain, which believed the illusion. It took her three months and some lessons with her truck before she chose to see the illusion for what it was. She made the unconscious choice to suffer, to not see through the illusion, to get the lessons about how those illusions, unwise choices, and thought energy impact the inanimate objects in her life."

Aidian chuckled. "Blaze, her truck, had been her indicator of where she stands with the male relationships in her life. On a four-hour trip, her thoughts about a particular gentleman who was part of the storm impacted Blaze's transmission, so he got 'bucky,' which reflected how Beth was feeling about that gentleman. Three weeks later, she recognized the illusion from the storm for what its true purpose was: a shield to protect her—the warrior in her was storming."

Star purr-laughed. "Beth does not like to be protected. If the, ahem, 'gentleman' who cast the illusion had instead chosen to use his language skills and trust, much of the conflict between them could have been avoided. That choice being made, events played out. I know Beth has learned her lessons, I hope he has as well."

"His guides are doing the best they can with him," Aidian replied.

"The truck and gentleman thing didn't end there, did it?" Filly asked.

"No, it didn't," Star replied. "Three weeks after she awoke from the illusion, Beth was driving Blaze home after a real snow storm. Hmm, see the pattern? Her patience with other drivers was almost gone, and that's when the accident happened. Blaze found a patch of ice, started fishtailing, and hit his left side on a bridge three times."

"Was Beth hurt? What about Blaze?" Pandy asked.

"The insurance company said Blaze was a total loss," Star said. "It would cost more to fix him than he was monetarily worth."

"Beth was physically fine. However, her heart was breaking to lose her truck," Aidian said. "She realized that losing Blaze was about letting go. Just as the water disaster was about flow, losing Blaze was about letting go of the past, letting her love flow first to her, then letting her love go to others. And, knowing when to let go of things you care about, even when it breaks your heart."

"So," Pandy asked, "Beth realized that in letting Blaze go, she was letting go of the gentleman she connected to the truck?"

"Correct," Aidian replied. "Letting go of both at the same time let her grieve and forgive. Now she can move on with the new truck she named Taezen, and make room for someone else in her life."

Filly stood up, stretched, chased her tail for a few moments, and asked, "So, we know where Beth has been. What do we know about her future? What can we do to help her?"

"She has to make the choices. We can help guide her to the right choices. But in the end, it's up to her, right?" asked Pandy.

"Choices," Aidian confirmed. "It's all about choices. Beth has made unwise choices in the past due to not having the tools she needed. She got by with what she had. Now she has more tools to help her make decisions. She's actively using her intuition, double-checking by testing kinesthetically before she makes major decisions. Even minor decisions, like where to get gas and what to do next, she asks about."

Filly stamped her paw, as much as a desert fox can, saying, "That still doesn't tell me anything! Choices! How, as one of her spirit guides, can I help her?" She sat down and thought for a moment, her head down. "Or can I?"

Aidian walked over and nuzzled Filly. "We wouldn't be here if we couldn't help her, little one. Beth made a choice to let each of us into her life, to be a connection to a part of her she couldn't see. You are her as a child, asking questions, listening for answers with those ears of yours." Aidian paused as Filly looked at him. "She loves you because you can hear so well, and she knows she doesn't always listen to herself, her intuition, or others. You remind her to listen."

"What about you?" Filly questioned. "What are you to her, Aidian?"

"I am what I am: a fox. I'm crafty, cunning, smart, and most of all, alive. I represent what Beth needed to survive until now. I provided wise council at times, especially when she first became aware of me. Now I'm her storyteller, telling of what was, and what could be."

"We are her dual nature," Thai said.

". . . We represent warrior and healer, male and female, private and public, the either/or situations in her life," Zen added. "Our colors, black and white, represent the either/or nature as well. There is very little gray in us, or in Beth's life. Things are, or are not. Quantum Physics depends on the moment of measurement, all possibilities are present until measured."

"Hey, that's my line," Star growled. "I'm her leveler and cat-alyst." He chuckled in amusement at his own pun. "Well, I am her catalyst, the one element that will spark the reaction to make the leap. Leap she has, this last year is proof for her that cause does not equal effect, and a system's reaction does not have to be in proportion to the amount of energy put into it.

"Beth's personal system, her body and brain, were ready to make changes. We saw how a simple gesture could cascade a reaction all out of proportion to that gesture. She, as a system, was waiting for the input, the trigger, a catalyst, to help her system make the leaps in faith, trust, and learning. She's received those triggers, inside and outside of her class. Once she understood her personal system, how the larger system of the world worked began to make sense."

"That is where I come in," Pandy said. "I reveal things to Beth, bringing things forth from unconscious to conscious. She can make those leaps. However, until she reveals to herself what those leaps mean to her, they do not matter. How many times has Beth made a leap with profound implications, then blown it off afterward? I help her see what she means, to herself, her soul, those she comes in contact with, and the world.

"I also help her 'see' the unseen world. Physical Human eyes have a limited range of vision. Beth has an awareness, a 'second sight' of energy fields around the body, the energy of spirits like her parents. When she's ready, I will reveal more to her."

Filly took all of this information in. "How does Beth's story end, Aidian?"

The red fox looked at the white filial fox for a moment, then replied, "Her story doesn't end here, Filly. Beth figures she has at least 50 more years in this lifetime, so in many ways her story is just beginning."

"Just beginning?" Filly asked. "She's almost 37. For most people that's half their lifetime, not the beginning."

"True enough, Filly," Aidian replied. "For *most* people. Beth isn't most people. She is a wise spirit who isn't letting the age of her current body hide the wisdom and knowledge of her previous lifetimes. She has claimed the mantle of healer, as she has many times before. Her warrior side still has a place, doing 'battle' per se with those whose understanding of alternative healing practices is hindered by their fear of the unknown. Education is her blade of choice. The more she knows, the wiser choices she can make, the more she can help guide others through their inner world to solve their own issues and problems."

"Our work with Beth is far from over," Star commented as he rose to his feet. "We have much to do, from helping her with her business, preparing her for her mate, building that dream house of hers, starting her foundations for all the things she wants to do. . ." Star's voice trailed off as he and the rest of the guides moved from their meeting area to another part of the valley.

Sleepy eyes opened as first one cat, then another bounced onto the bed, rousing her out of her dream. "Hey, you two," she said to the cats, Rainbow and Shadow. "I was in the middle of this great dream, a story my animal guides were telling about my life." As Beth continued on, Rainbow looked at Shadow and winked.

I would like to thank The Meta Institute (www.metainstitute.com) and Class C. These 21 people have made a profound impact on my life over the last 13 months. I am most grateful for them to have shared this part of my journey.

About
Beth Kopitzke

Beth Kopitzke became interested in coaching as a profession after working for two years with a coach. Earlier, she had experienced a wide range of career pathways that led her to pursue massage therapy as a vocation. She attended the Minneapolis School of Massage and Bodywork, completing the massage practitioner and sports massage curriculums during 1995-96. For a few years she owned a massage therapy business. Once Beth became intrigued by the coaching profession, she attended the Coach Training Institute's Co-Active Coaching Course, and opened a small practice from her home.

Beth continued her professional development at the Meta Institute for Certified Therapeutic Coach® Training in 2003. There she learned about Neuro-Linguistic Programming (NLP), humanistic neuro-linguistic psychology, Ericksonian hypnosis, Quantum Physics, systems work, and more, also becoming a second level Reiki practitioner. She has taken Spring Forest Qigong levels one and two from Master Chunyi Lin, and intends to complete levels three and four. She continues to take advanced level courses in NLP and hypnosis to further her knowledge and understanding of how we as human beings work.

Beth specializes in combining the therapeutic coaching, massage therapy, and energy work to help people who are interested in and ready to heal themselves, body, mind, and spirit. Through several avenues for healing, she assists clients who come to her with an issue or problem, either in their body or in their lives. In the body, massage therapy works out the "issues in the tissues," bringing memories stored in the muscles, fascia, and structure to the surface. In their lives, therapeutic coaching takes those memories, along with old emotions, beliefs, values, and outcomes, and using the client's language, accesses the brain's neurology, unconscious, and higher conscious minds to resolve those issues. Reiki and Qigong energy work assists the physical and energetic bodies and minds in healing themselves.

Beth currently resides in the western suburbs of the Minneapolis-St. Paul metro area, along with her two cats, Rainbow and Shadow, her truck Taezen and motorcycle Hawk.

To contact Beth, email befwin@goldengate.net, call 763-553-7847, or visit www.InquireWithinHealing.com.

A Journey to Trust the Universe

By Lisa Matzke

"Our lives begin to end the day we become silent about things that matter." ~ Dr. Martin Luther King Jr.

Time just stopped. I don't know how long I was there, crying and asking God to wake him up, not believing that this was happening. Stuart was thirty-eight. He couldn't die. I wasn't even aware that I was crying until someone gave me a tissue. My stepfather observed that it looked like Stuart was looking at me, and he was right. Stuart's eyes were slightly open and there were tears, like he was crying too. Like he didn't want to die. He loved his little family. We were so excited about our life and all of our plans. Skiing, moving to the sun, not working so much, and enjoying raising CJ and having another baby. But all of our dreams stopped and died that night. I was to start anew and create my own dreams, learn to be on my own, learn to step into my own shoes, to be a leader, as Stuart was a leader in his field, and to heal myself. To raise CJ, go to school, start my own business. And most importantly, to stand up for myself. I wasn't able to look back and see Stuart's death as a gift until years later. And it wasn't until years later that I'd be able to do any of those things that led me to see that gift.

My journey to trust—in myself and the universe—started on November 24th, 1997. That day I had returned from a major shopping excursion in preparation for Thanksgiving. This would be my first time cooking and having my in-laws to my home for the holiday. My son, CJ, who was 16 months at the time, was trying to lift the gallon milk jug. The gesture, which mimicked my husband's workouts in our spare bedroom, was so cute that I called Stuart at his office to share the moment. Although he was the president of his company, he still made time for me when I called to update him on our son's many accomplishments. He so enjoyed hearing about anything CJ or I was doing.

Later that night, after putting our baby to sleep, Stuart left to play basketball with his buddies, as he did every Monday night. He had started to play in preparation for the ski season, to get in shape for racing. He had commented a few weeks earlier that basketball was a great sport for getting in shape, but that it might kill him. Later I remembered that prophetic statement.

The night before was also very prophetic. CJ woke up crying. This might have been usual for most parents, but what wasn't usual was that I was unable to rock him to sleep. Over an hour I tried to get CJ to sleep, but every time I'd put him back in his crib he'd start crying again. Finally I joined my husband, saying I didn't know what to do and maybe he needed to cry himself to sleep. Stuart got up without saying anything and went to CJ. Within moments all was quiet. I tiptoed down the hall and peered in the room. Father and son were staring at each other and Stuart was quietly talking to his baby. It was such an incredibly beautiful sight, the connection and love they were sharing. I know that CJ knew at that time, but he couldn't talk.

Around 9:00 that Monday night, the phone rang. Andy, a friend of Stuart's on the basketball team, said the words that would change my life. "Stuart's had a heart attack!" My first thought was that he's joking. A split second later, I yelled in a shocked voice, "Tell him that I love him." Andy replied, "They're working on him."

I called my parents, who lived down the street. While my mother watched CJ, my stepfather raced me at speeds over 100 in my mom's new Mercedes to Stuart. On the thirty-minute drive to the gymnasium, we were pulled over by a policeman. When he allowed us to continue, he followed us for a short time, probably not believing our emergency was real. He must have verified our story because he suddenly pulled in front of us with his lights and siren on and escorted us to the school.

The days after Stuart's death were surreal. Viewing my husband in a casket, knowing he would not have wanted to have his body viewed, but doing it anyway, desperate not to be parted from him. I joked with his sister about how goofy he looked with the way they'd styled his hair. I went through the motions as I made decisions: what casket, what urn, having his body cremated. There were little things, like losing his license, thinking that the funeral home had it. I wanted it for a memento for CJ, but wasn't able to call the funeral home for it. I was freaking out inside, but wasn't able to tell anyone else about how I was feeling, because the feelings were nothing that I'd ever felt. I had no experience up to this point with death on a personal level.

The darkness started to creep in. Every day it got worse, where nothing and no one could ease the pain. Before Stuart's death I had believed in God. I had prayed to spare his life and I had been denied. I couldn't understand why God would take Stuart away from his son and wife. I felt betrayed and abandoned and I railed at God. The darkness continued. There were no words that could describe the pain I felt. There were times I would collapse physically, bruising my body. Mentally, I felt I'd go crazy not being able to talk to Stuart, not being able to hear his voice or feel him next to me. We were so much in love, waking up entwined, sometimes laughing and wondering if our loving had been a dream or real.

Before his death, Stuart and I had been looking for a church that we both like. Neither of us was involved in the religions or churches that we'd been brought up in and were searching for our special place. We felt a need to have spirituality in a very material world. We knew we wanted balance in all areas of our lives. After we had visited one church shortly before he died, he had surprised me by asking me to marry him again when we finally found "our" church. We were still looking when he died.

Although I felt abandoned by God, I continued to talk to him, with one recurring thought moving me in those dark days: I begged to be with Stuart again. At first, I only thought of me dying. Then I begged God to take both CJ and me. My overriding desire was for us to be together as our happy little family again.

Immediately after he died, Stuart started to visit me. After the funeral, I had gone to Mexico with my family. CJ and I were in bed, and he was fast asleep. I was awake in the pitch-dark room. I noticed first sort of a mist, or fog right above me, not very many inches from my face. It was lightish in color. And then I felt Stuart's body laying on top of me, from my toes to my lips. Somehow he let me know that I wouldn't be able to move my body except my head. The experience was strange, but not scary. I turned my head toward CJ, and his face changed to Stuart's. Then he spoke to me: "I didn't want to die, I miss you and I love you." I felt then both the complete love that I had felt when he was alive, and the conflicting feelings of the pain of his death.

Stuart continued to visit me and I found myself living for those moments, for they brought me comfort. For the brief time he came, my pain was eased. Days slowly turned to weeks and then months. The darkness continued to submerge me and little tasks became huge. Every day I fell behind a little more. I tried to read, hoping that it would ease the pain, wanting something that would allow me to avoid thinking or feeling about Stuart's death and the unbearable pain I was experiencing. Although I had been a voracious reader, I found it difficult to focus on the words.

There were, however, two books that came to me during this time that helped tremendously. One, *The Eagle and the Rose*, by Rosemary Altea, mysteriously appeared on our dresser after Stuart's death. He had read this book after his mom died and before we had moved into our house, and it gave him great comfort. The other book was *Talking to Heaven* by James Van Praagh. Both of these books have given me immense comfort. At the time, I was still living in a place of fear and darkness, and so was unaware of the spiritual connection these books could also provide.

Running became the only thing that I could count on to relieve the pain. And so I ran. I ran my first marathon a year after Stuart's death. I ran it in honor of Stuart. He'd always wanted to run a marathon, so I did. It was a wonderful experience and as I was running up the last hill passing people, I knew that Stuart was with me. I came through the finish line with my arms raised in celebration. The experience was a complete high and one that I thought I could never accomplish. I thought that you had to be special to run a marathon. Running would become my primary form of escaping, a coping mechanism, a way to survive. I began to do anything that required physical endurance: a 200-mile bike ride, which I did in a day; triathlons; some days I'd ride my bike 40 miles, jump off, and run another 12 miles. Then I'd go about my day, reading to CJ, playing with him, meeting his needs.

Stuart also gave me signs of our connection through heart rocks. It started when CJ and I visited our beach property that Stuart and I had bought before our son was born. CJ and I were celebrating Stuart's birthday by enjoying a picnic on the beach. We were walking when CJ gave me a rock. I looked at it and noticed that it was the shape of a heart. We played a game of who could find the most heart rocks. CJ found three and I couldn't find any. After that day CJ would always find heart rocks and give them to me, and soon I was able to find them too.

At one point, we went to visit Lake Ann, a beautiful lake where I had scattered Stuart's ashes. Stuart, CJ, and I had hiked the gorgeous trail there the summer before he'd died. We had so much fun, with CJ on Stuart's back as we slid down the glacier. That day instilled in me a love for hiking, one of Stuart's favorite activities. The incredible beauty of the hike, the fact that this trail helped me to appreciate hiking, made it the most fitting place to scatter his ashes. As CJ and I hiked there for the third time, all along the way I saw heart rocks. In one section of the hike, where we traversed through sheer rocks, every step I took seemed to be on a rock in the shape of a heart. The experience was so amazing. I knew then that I was spiritually supported and Stuart was connecting with me clearly, encouraging me to follow my heart.

Another occasion that gave me assurance that I had spiritual support was when a friend stopped by with a pink heart quartz crystal. She saw it and thought of me, not knowing that the day was my wedding anniversary, or that Stuart had given me the exact crystal heart in a vision I had just a few months earlier.

∗ ∗ ∗

Everyone told me that "time heals all wounds." How wrong they were. During those dark days of wandering, waiting for time to fast forward so I could leave the pain, I felt like I was stumbling along outside in the dark, not knowing where to go or who to turn to. When a friend set me up on a date with this "great guy," I instinctively knew to stay away from this man, but I chose to ignore my inner warnings. I was lost, tired, and had given up. It was so easy for him to get a hold of me. I call this period of my grieving "having my head buried in sand like an ostrich." I was not willing to see what was occurring around me. Maybe it was because my heart was of the light, my naivety, my belief that because I wouldn't hurt someone intentionally, someone wouldn't hurt me. I knew that a deep darkness, an evilness existed, more in some people than others, but I didn't believe it could or would touch me. But, along with losing my identity as a result of my husband's death, my boundaries became unclear and I became an easy target. I didn't believe that a man proclaiming to love me would actually hate me and want to end my life and my son's. He was a smooth talker, good looking, and had an ability to be a chameleon, as he had bragged to me. I remember feeling scared and sickened when he had shared this with me. But for some reason, I couldn't see to get out of the relationship. The experience was like being in the middle of a hurricane, where, in the eye of the storm, I couldn't see the destruction that this man was causing.

Looking back now, I know that I was scared from the day Stuart died. But by keeping my head buried, as I told my teacher later, the environment around me began to escalate. The more I ignored the universe, the more it knocked on my door. I was afraid of moving through the door, and I felt it was easier and safer to settle. So settle I did. I stayed with this "great guy" and told myself all kinds of stories and convinced myself that he was true to me, that he was my knight in shining armor. I stayed because I thought that being with him was better than being alone.

What a paradox. I had gone from an ultimate love relationship to the polar opposite. Even my son, who was by that time five years old, said, "Don't marry him; he has a black heart." I continued to ignore my inner warnings and those from family and friends.

What saved me from continuing on the road to destruction was, simply put, Stuart. One beautiful sunny day in August 2002, I left my son at home with the housekeeper and went to a scheduled healing session. I had told the housekeeper that I would be gone an hour and a half, at the most.

The session wasn't progressing well. I was stuck and couldn't seem to let go or to move back or forward. All of a sudden, I was in the entry of my new home and this "great guy" entered and proceeded to stab me repeatedly and kill me. In the trance-like state that I was in, I was gasping and at the same time floating above my body in the entry, as I looked down on blood everywhere. The healer was next to me and I could sense her panic. She asked me if I could call on anyone spiritually. I called out to Stuart and immediately he appeared next to me on the left side. I could see him clearly standing there and he touched my arm with his hand. He said, "Lisa, trust the universe." And then he was gone. The session was over, and I was worried because it was well past two hours since I had been there. The healer was still very concerned and asked if I needed to call the police. I was so unnerved by the events that had so quickly developed that I vaguely said no, everything was okay, and hurried home.

I'd been given a picture of what could happen if I chose to stay with this man. I was also given support from the universe to trust—and to walk away from this guy—to walk through the door the universe had opened for me, to walk through without knowing what was on the other side. Where I would move from being dependant on someone else, to being independent, and finally interdependent.

I called the police to protect myself, for the "great guy's" actions became extremely deviant and I knew my life was in danger. The police concurred with me and urged me to break contact with this man.

Stuart had planted a seed and it took hold. I had gone home from that healing session wondering what the heck did he mean? I had never heard that phrase "trust the universe." That eye-opener was the turning point that helped me start the next part of my journey, to healing my heart, trusting myself, and empowering myself with the universe's love—God's love. Stuart's death was the door to becoming independent. This turning point opened the door to becoming conscious.

After the healing session, I started reading everything I could get my hands on, self-help, spiritual, and inspirational. Some of the books practically jumped off the shelf at me, and the very supportive people in my life recommended more. The first very insightful and noteworthy book was *The Verbally Abusive Relationship* by Patricia Evans. Her writing described the man I was with, our relationship, and also the co-creative relationship that I had with my husband. I jubilantly called my friends and family, sharing with them my discovery. The next book I read was *Feel the Fear and Do It Anyway* by Susan Jeffers, which inspired me to courageously walk away and obtain a restraining order against this man. After that there was no stopping me. The weight was lifted. Soon after, I ran my third marathon and it felt incredible. I compared the years spent with the "great guy" like running a marathon every day with a 180 pound man on my back. I was free and light and enjoyed being a workshop junkie, going to classes and support groups, and reading books. I received my certification in coaching, angel therapy, and spiritual medium-ship, Neuro-Linguistic Programming, and Paradox Management. In the process I learned many tools that supported me in healing my heart, in becoming conscious. And I had many opportunities to apply these tools on myself. The new knowledge supported me as I moved through the grief of my husband's death and subsequent abuse from my boyfriend. What I learned was that I could not replace Stuart or "get over it," but that I could acknowledge and feel the pain of both experiences.

I was on the path to healing when I went to a special event at my church that I had found years after Stuart and I were looking. They were holding a celebration for the loss of loved ones. I felt until then that I had completely healed, so it took me by surprise what unfolded that night. As I sat in the pew with all the stuffed animals that were donated for children in need, I picked up this sweet little dog who had the most compelling eyes. I held him during the meditation given by the minister. I continued holding him as I summoned my angels and guides. I called the Archangels for healing, protection, courage, and strength into the space with me. I allowed myself to feel the pain of losing Stuart. Oh, and it hurt! There was a box of Kleenex next to me and I let myself cry.

The minister asked for people to share their story, and as much as I wanted to, I couldn't because the tears and pain were so much for me. Almost too much, but I knew that I was safe and so I continued to cry. I cried so much that when I arrived home later I took out all the tissue from my pockets and purse and it made a mound on the counter.

As I sat in the church, I held on to my little dog. Something in the dog's eyes reminded me of Stuart, as if Stuart was telling me to transfer my pain to the dog. As I sat in the pew soundlessly talking to Stuart, I told him how much I loved him, but I needed and wanted to be whole and complete, so I was allowing Archangel Michael to cut the remaining cord connecting us. I wanted to be free of the pain of his death and I wanted Stuart to be whole and complete, too.

When I got home late that night, I washed my hands. I looked at the soap, and you know when the soap gets wet and stays wet it turns white? That white was in the perfect shape of a heart. I knew that Stuart was showing me a sign of his love. I felt it was an acknowledgement of the love between us, and recognition of the incredibly hard and courageous work I'd completed.

* * *

I knew then that I was ready to help others heal, too. One of my overriding themes of my business is that there is no "getting over it!" Our society teaches us to just get over a loss. I feel that this is very harmful to people wanting to heal their hearts, heal from the loss of a loved one or the death of a favorite pet, a divorce, a breakup of a friendship, loss of a job. We are told to move on, replace the loss, buck up, you have to be strong for others, etc. I say no, acknowledge the loss. Acknowledging the horror of the situation validates the grief that the person is experiencing. Don't try to change the situation by saying "time heals all wounds" or other words of consolation.

What helped me more were times like when my doctor sent me a card a few months after Stuart had died. In it she said, "I hope you're surviving." That was all. Such simple words.

There are so many tools that will allow you to feel that pain, to go inside it, to find out what the message is that resides there for you, the pearl of wisdom that shows you how to move through it. I believe you must do that to truly heal and to let go of those past experiences. And I now share the tools that worked for me with my clients as I support them on their journey to trusting the universe.

The outcome of my journey is that now I believe that God is love—more love than I can possibly imagine. Love that is unbiased and accepting, without fear or blame. Fear is what we humans place on our selves and others. It's debilitating and destructive. Everyone has the light of God within. People *choose* to live in fear, which shadows that light. The more fear, the more shadows. And as those shadows grow, they attract more distrust, more anger, more hate into our lives.

Along my journey the light in my heart cut through the layers of distrust and hurt. Using those tools the universe provided along the way, I allowed the layers of darkness to fall away. The tools supported me in my soul's evolution, my path to consciousness, my healing my heart, my journey to enlightenment. There are many labels or names for this work. A word of warning: This path isn't easy. However, neither is unconsciousness. Both are work. And once you become conscious, there is no going back. But which would you rather live with, darkness and fear, or love and light?

In my own experience becoming conscious through the grief process, I sometimes feel that my knowledge and understanding of my core identity is continually trying to catch up with my soul, which is miles ahead of me. The journey can be scary. Since becoming aware that I am on a path to the light, what I believe in can change day to day and moment to moment. What I've come to believe is that there are many levels of reality. And while fear is normal and part of all of us, it does not have to be a dominant factor in our current reality.

What is important on this spiritual path is discernment and flexibility. What works for one person might not work for another. However, there is one area where there must be no flexibility. When working with the forces of the universe, you must set a clear, strong boundary to only allow light and love into your life. State your intentions clearly. The universe will give you what you ask for, so be specific.

Here are some of the tools that work for me. You can choose to implement them into your routine or not. You're at choice...

I now know how to trust the universe with shielding, connecting to God through prayer and meditation. The following ritual I enjoy doing upon awakening. I do this every day, and yes, at first it was difficult. But when I do this, I feel so alive, joyful, and have so much inner peace.

Upon awakening in the morning, first ask your angels, guides, and the archangels to protect yourself and your loved ones, then quietly visualize the light of the universe shining down through the top of your head, all through your body, touching every cell with its healing light. Then bring up the light from the heart of mother earth all through your body, touching every cell with its healing and loving energy. Then allow this light to radiate out of your heart. This beautiful luminescent white light is now surrounding and shielding your body from negativity and transmuting any anger—directed at either yourself or others—to love. Picture this shield at arm's length from your body, hold out your arm with palm facing away just like you were saying stop. This is where your shield is and you've anchored it. Now move this light further from your body, so your room is bathed in this pure white light of the universe. Continue breathing deeply, completely relaxed. Next, move the light throughout your home and everyone in it, touching all your loved ones. Continue moving the light throughout your neighborhood, city, state, country, and throughout the world, touching everyone you know with light.

Throughout the day picture yourself enclosed in a translucent bubble, like those you would blow from a child's bubble-making toy. The luminous bubble allows only love and light to flow from it and into it. All else is transmuted. For extra protection when going into crowded places, you can place an outer shield so that negativity does not penetrate the circle. You can set the intention that all negativity is reflected back and transmuted to love. Or visualize angels carrying away the negative energy and giving it to the light, where it's transmuted to love.

Death and, believe it or not, feeling the sensations of pain, opened me up to light. I learned that endings are beginnings and beginnings are endings. Each occurs to allow for the other to happen. To keep things still or the way they were is like trying to stop a river from flowing.

Because of unexpected journeys—and with support and love from the universe—I was able to see that I am a healer, a spiritual teacher. With my own, new-found power and the power of those who have gone on before me, I now know my purpose is to better our world by empowering people to move to the light—to trust the universe and to open our hearts to all that is possible in that light.

About
Lisa Matzke

Lisa Matzke is a Spiritual Teacher and Personal Performance Coach. She has studied with Ragini Michaels on paradox and the psychology of the mystics. As a graduate of Ragini Michaels' Paradox School of Wisdom, Lisa learned how to effectively engage on both practical and spiritual levels. Lisa also earned her certification in Neuro-Linguistic Programming (NLP) with Ragini Michaels.

In early 2004, Lisa received her International Life Coaching Certificate from the Academy of Coach Training in Bellevue Washington. In addition, Lisa received certification as an Angel Therapy Practitioner and Spiritual Medium-ship from nationally renowned psychologist and best-selling author, Dr. Doreen Virtue.

In addition to these trainings, Lisa integrates powerful intuitive gifts in her personal coaching practice. She helps clients move through obstacles, instead of trying to "get over" them. She teaches trusting the universe, and instructs on how to obtain and recognize doors the universe provides to manifest your desired life—a life of freedom, a life of quality, a life filled with light and love.

Lisa is sharing her experiences since her husband's death in workshops that empower her audiences to trust themselves and the universe.

To contact Lisa, call 206-232-6444, email info@lisamatzke.com, or visit www.LisaMatzke.com.

To order more copies of this book or for more information
about the series, visit:
www.AGuideToGettingIt.com
or call 503-460-0014.

For more information about Clarity of Vision, Inc., and the
work that we do, visit www.ClarityofVision.com.

With Best Regards,
Marilyn Schwader
President and Founder
Clarity of Vision, Inc.